ALL QUIET ON THE RUSSIAN FRONT

Sept 18/75

ALL QUIET ON THE RUSSIAN FRONT

by
KURT W. STOCK

A POCKET BOOK EDITION published by
Simon & Schuster of Canada, Ltd. ● Richmond Hill, Ontario, Canada
Registered User of the Trademark

With the exception of my own, all the names of people in this book have been changed. They are, nevertheless, real people and their stories are true.

ALL QUIET ON THE RUSSIAN FRONT

One of a series of original Canadian books first published by Simon & Schuster of Canada, Limited.
Editor — Jock Carroll
POCKET BOOK edition published May 1973

Cover painting by Andy Donato

This original POCKET BOOK edition is printed from brand-new plates made from newly set, clear, easy-to-read type. POCKET BOOK editions are published by POCKET BOOKS, a division of Simon & Schuster of Canada, Ltd., 225 Yonge Street North, Richmond Hill, Ontario.
Trademarks registered in Canada and other countries.

ALL QUIET ON THE
RUSSIAN FRONT

CHAPTER ONE

Towards the end of February 1945, Infantry Regiment 307 was caught in the depths of a heavily forested area to the north of Pomerania, a province in east Germany. Other units were with us in the same area, fragments of a battered force, which until now had been harassed on all sides by Russian gunfire. Now, the sounds of battle had ceased. A tactical delay had given us a brief respite.

We had gone without sleep for several days; the Russian onslaught had continued without let-up, throwing great strength against our weary forces. We were the remnants of a fighting force that had seen service on the Finnish front, but astronomical losses in men and material had almost destroyed us.

The oppressive silence served as an added burden to our spirits; leaving us in a state of confusion, as murderous perhaps as bullets.

Then the message came, scouts returning from all directions left no doubt as to the grim picture. *Eingeschlossen!* [We were surrounded.] Our eavy artillery had stopped supporting us. Perhaps it was already dismantled.

The news of our situation caused much dissension in an extraordinarily brave company. For four years we had fought through thick and thin, and the men had never reacted like this.

On the front in Finland we learned to endure forced marches, close encounters with the enemy, and massive assaults. In the brutal winter of 1941, we survived the nerve-shattering trench warfare. All of this, and more, we

1

withstood with honor and distinction. We had sustained heavy losses before, and our fighting spirit never wavered. It was our sacred duty to keep the enemy away from the Fatherland.

But now the picture was different; our morale was broken. The victories of yesterday had been replaced by defeats and *"Frontverkuerzungen"*. Exhaustion, depletion of our units, battle fatigue, and an endless series of defeats made us completely war-weary.

A man does not have to be a military genius to know that the grenade in his launcher is a dud. Likewise, when the common soldier began to think militarily, it was a dangerous sign. Frederick the Great said, "If my soldiers begin to think, I will have no more soldiers".

No one spoke openly about our situation; in the brief exchanges which passed for conversation, there was no mention of defeat. But everyone, who had two eyes in his head could see it written on our vacant, hollow-cheeked faces.

I was twenty-four. *Obergefreiter* (Senior Lance Corporal) Kurt Stock. I was only twenty when they called me to serve, and I never questioned my duty. But now, doubt passed through my head as I sat checking my automatic pistol in preparation for the coming battle.

"They really want to drive us through Hell!" I muttered.

One question kept churning around in my head. Where in damnation was this breakthrough supposed to lead us?

The platoon messenger came running by, calling the group leaders together. I reported to Ober Feldwebel (Sergeant-Major) Schneider. His throat was hoarse with over-excitement.

I should have guessed it. Our platoon, as usual, won the grand prize. We had been chosen to spearhead the breakthrough. Our job would be to ram a wedge into the enemy lines, enabling the rest of the company to follow.

Sergeant Schneider made an attempt to bolster our

confidence, but the truth was written in his chalky face and in the assignment he gave us. Perhaps he already knew this was to be his last command, because leading us away, he merely said, "Good luck."

Our group led the way and began drawing the enemy fire. A rain of bullets and shells fell on us from every side. I saw Sergeant Schneider lying on the forest floor, his limbs hanging lifelessly together. He had taken a bullet in the head.

Then the Doors of Hell opened up when they brought in their heavy armaments against us — mortar, artillery and everything else they had, firing with frightening accuracy. We lay in a trough, convinced that this was our last moment on earth. A sustained drive was out of the question because the next group followed us too closely; they ran directly into the enemy fire and were slaughtered immediately. Casualties were mounting while chaos prevailed. Our breakthrough failed miserably and with it our hope of escape.

It was a miracle that so many of us survived under the direct fire of the Russians. Luckily, they did not pursue their advantage; they were satisfied that we sat in a trap.

There were only two dead from our group of nine; we had suffered relatively light casualties. Words were unnecessary to describe how we felt, since we all understood.

The failure of our mission revealed to us the true wretchedness of our condition. Men were racing up and down like animals in a cage, and when the order to reassemble was given, we moved like condemned men.

Captain Weinrich, the company chief, stood with the batallion commander on a small hill. When the captain began to speak, I imagined at first that I heard incorrectly. He spoke of our past heroism and about the bitter fighting in Finland. When he came to our present situation, he was short and direct. Our own resources were completely spent and it was futile to hold out under these conditions. He stressed each word, and speaking quietly and solemnly, ended by saying:

"*Kameraden!* I hereby dissolve the Third Company. The war is over for you. You may have the liberty of deciding whether to go to prison, or seek freedom on your own. I personnally believe you will be more successful in slipping between the enemy lines if you work in small groups. What your chances are, on one can say. Whatever you decide to do, my parting wish is: Good luck, good-bye, and a safe return to your loved ones."

These words did not penetrate at once, and we stood without moving, like deaf men. Yet, as the message came through — for us the war is over! — we gradually became animated, full of nervous vitality. Arms and hands crossed back and forth in every direction — our motions were jerky, like puppets on a string.

I began the march with two buddies. Walter Novak was a machine gunner and private first class and Karl Behnke, a private. Both were from my group. We had been together a long time, seeing plenty of action. We were all about the same age, and decided not to go to prison no matter what. We also made plans for the march. We would try to stay together, and march by night, resting by day.

We were all convinced of one thing. Our only hope of escape lay in the direction of the Baltic Sea.

Before we left, Walter, the comedian among us said, "Wait you guys!"

He removed the lock from his machine gun, throwing it far away. With a sly twinkle in his hazel eyes, while making an unmistakable gesture, he said, "So! At least Ivan won't be able to shoot me in the ass with my own machine gun!"

Karl and I chuckled; then we followed his example. We also got rid of our helmets, gas masks and field spades. Naturally, we held on to our rifles and automatics.

Late I discovered that Karl still was in possession of his gas mask. When I gave him a mystified look, he grinned and waved his hands as if he were warding off smoke. I understood. The box was full of cigarettes, an old soldier's trick for protecting tobacco from dampness.

It was getting dark, and high time to be off.

"Well, you two," I croaked, "Let's get the hell out of here!"

Many of our comrades we would never see again. We learned later that the batallion commander and our company chief had ended their own lives by putting a bullet into their heads.

As I was the only one with a compass, I took the lead. It was good weather for starting off. The sky was overcast, there was no moon to expose us to the Russian sentries. The fresh layer of snow gave us just enough light to proceed without stumbling on the forest floor, and in a short time, we were covered by the dense blanket of trees.

We moved toward the west for a time, the opposite direction of the breakthrough. After walking for about a half hour, we began to circle around.

We had to proceed very slowly because the night carried sounds from every part of the forest. Shots were heard to the left — we froze in our tracks. There was the answering report of a machine gun. Then silence. We began moving slowly again. Later on, we heard twigs snapping close by. We halted and listened — nothing. Our senses had been sharpened by years of training.

We moved along for quite some time without incident. Suddenly I gave the signal to halt. Instantly, we were down on our stomachs, hugging the snow. Something was moving in the bushes directly before us — there it was again ! Was it a face I saw ?

Walter crept up beside me, "What's up ?"

I pointed toward a bush. In the awful silence, my heart beat so loudly, I was sure they heard it in Moscow. My eyes were burning from the prolonged strain of peering into the overcast night. But there was some comfort in this because if I couldn't see Ivan, neither could he see me.

Ever so slowly, on rubbery legs, Walter, Karl and I crept backwards for several yards. When I felt we were out of danger, I hid behind a tree and stood up, my automatic poised, ready to shoot.

Karl rushed up to me.

I exclaimed, "A Russian sentry's there! I'm sure of it!"

Walter suggested, "Perhaps we're beginning to see ghosts. Bushes can assume any shape in such light!"

"Safety is safety!" Karl murmured philosophically. "Come on. Let's get out of here."

Luck was with us; it began snowing, and thick, moist, beautiful snow flakes dropped gently to the ground, obscuring us completely.

In the distance, we could hear the sound of machine gun fire, interspersed with single shots. We became bolder, walking more swiftly now, continuing in the northerly direction without further incident. After hiking a few more hours, we took refuge in some underbrush.

I could hardly withstand the desire for a cigarette, but it was still too dangerous to risk striking a match. We broke into our rations, munching on hardtack while we huddled together for warmth and protection. We were in a cold and lonely part of the world, surrounded by enemies. We felt like orphans, completely abandoned by man and nature.

Almost prostrate with fatigue, we agreed it was essential to find an adequate shelter before dawn. That is to say, when I told Walter and Karl we couldn't stay here, they grumbled and cursed. I took this as a sign of agreement, and we started up again, continuing in the same direction.

It seemed as if the forest was getting brighter. Suddenly I realized that we were coming to some sort of clearing. I listened for noise coming from the forest, but heard only our heavy breathing.

"What do you think ?" Walter asked, "Are we safe ?"

"I don't know Karl, what's your opinion ?"

"It seems peaceful enough." was all Karl said.

We decided to stay under cover and circle the field.

After about a mile, I saw a light shining in the bushes. It was a big camp fire. I crept up behind a tree, and I could see figures moving around — they did not appear to be Russians. Gaining some confidence, I worked myself closer. I could have danced with happiness because they were wearing German uniforms. I was certain, as soon as I heard them speaking.

I signalled to my two comrades that everything was alright. We shouted and waved to let them know that we were coming. Though we had exercised stealth and precaution all night, we were amazed to find a blazing campfire and a total lack of concern for the enemy. As Walter put it when he saw its welcoming light, "Hey ! Look what's here ! A real Indian campfire ! These guys act just like they own the forest !"

And Karl muttered, "Man, I've seen just about every-thing now !"

Seated around the campfire were about fifty German soldiers, all in the same wretched condition we were in. I recognized several men from our batallion; the others were strangers. We sat by the campfire, warming our hands. While now the much-craved cigarette was smoked. We learned here that Captain Weinrich and the batallion commander had shot themselves rather than face capture. Also, we were the remnants of different companies. The only officer here was a young lieutenant by the name of Siegfried Sommer; he was also the leader of the group.

When Walter heard this, he exclaimed, "I don't need a bloody Fuerher ! I need sleep !"

Surrounded by so many comrades, we felt secure and

crept in between the others, finding places for ourselves, and in no time at all, fell asleep.

Hours later, someone shook my arm, awakening me. "Hey. Wake up! You've slept enough!"

I sat up, rubbing my eyes. "What's the matter?"

The lieutenant wants to see you and your buddies. I'll take you to him."

I knew the man who spoke. He was Unteroffizier Schwarz of the Fourth Company. He glared down at us from above his full black beard. It was already broad daylight and the sky was clear and the sun shone brightly. The campsite was empty and no fire burned. We rolled up the blankets, took our weapons and followed Unteroffizier Schwarz.

The Lieutenant sat deep in concentration before a map, as Schwartz squatted beside him. After we gave the lieutenant our names, rank and regiment, he asked us to sit down.

"My name is Lieutenant Sommer, Regiment-Staff," he explained, "We are going to try to reach the Baltic Sea; do you wish to join us?"

As he asked this question, he scrutinized our faces, burning us with his blue eyes. For a few seconds, I was able to study his features. How young he was! His youthful face, blond hair, and fine nose, made such a contrast to the job he undertook!

I had to think quickly. Without any previous knowledge, I was inclined to dislike him. Could a young officer have the foresight, experience, and other leadership qualities necessary to hold together such a shabby, down-at-the-mouth group of soldiers, and bring them to freedom? My eyes sought those of Corporal Schwarz, who shrugged his shoulders.

Since Walter and Karl remained silent, it was up to me to think of an answer, at least for now.

"Jawohl Herr Lieutenant! We also wish to reach the Baltic." I paused, then continued weighing each word, "I believe that my two comrades and I will stay with you as long as the situation warrants it."

I could see that he did not consider my answer quite satisfactory, but he said,

"Good. You now belong to Corporal Schwarz's group." He pointed toward the Corporal.

"He is your group leader."

With calculated gestures, he indicated areas on the map,

"My scouts inform me that the Russians are in possession of the village of Pasenow. All roads leading to and from it are being guarded. Most probably all other towns and villages in the area are also occupied. The enemy is at present too busy holding the towns to bother with the forest, although special troops will, probably, be assigned to clean up the forests after these have moved on. I intend to move swiftly at night, resting during the day, under the cover of the forest. We will avoid all roads and highways; this takes longer, but is certainly a safer method of travelling."

He paused, taking a cigarette. We were glad to follow his example. Although we were no longer under military rule, the force of habit remained with us, and we observed the established protocol in the presence of a commanding officer. After a few tugs on his cigarette, he continued,

"We are in a desperate position with respect to provisions. Unfortunately, the forest and the neighboring fields do not yield anything to eat in winter. We have no alternative but to send raiding parties into the villages taking whatever we can find — by force if necessary." He dragged some more on his cigarette, "We have no time to lose because we're moving on as soon as it is dark. Our direction is due north, and during the night we'll pass several villages. If the opportunity is favorable, I will decide whether or not to undertake a raid."

He snuffed out his cigarette butt in the snow.

"That is all until your next orders. Unteroffizier

Schwarz, I'll relieve your group of guard duty for today because I want them to get a good rest, they're going to spearhead tonight's venture."

Life never changes, I thought.

Lieutenant Sommer concluded by saying, "I will put groups one and two at your disposal for wing protection. That is all."

We were dismissed.

The moment we were out of hearing range, Walter began to raise a fuss. I rammed him in the side and hissed through my teeth,

"Shut up, damn it! Later!"

Then I walked ahead of him so he could not talk to me any more. Schwarz said to Walter,

"Your pistol won't do for tonight. You'll need a rifle."

We came to the area where Group Three was situated, and I recognized three soldiers from my batallion. The others were strangers. Schwarz named me second in command. As briefly as possible, he informed the others of the night's foray. The information was poorly received. One private said,

"Piss on that! I don't like the risk. Besides, I can't stand violence." His neighbor added,

"Likewise for me. I faint easily at the sight of blood."

Walter could not stand it any longer. He said to us.

"Hurry up and follow me. We've got to collect some underbrush for our sack."

He dashed off into the forest, while Karl and I followed close behind.

As soon as we caught up with him, Walter began gesticulating, his arms revolving like the sails of a windmill, his huge eyes rolling like a butchered cow.

"You've both had enough time to take a good look at that lieutenant, haven't you?"

His eyes flashed in anger. Before we could utter a word, he continued,

"I know that type, alright; fresh from officer's school! A young punk like that's going to lead us all the way to the Baltic? I don't think he could walk a blind old lady across the street!"

"Relax, Walter! Calm down!"

Walter put his face close to mine and hissed,

"You want me to take it easy, while that bastard is pissing with ideas of dying a hero's death for Fuehrer, Volk and Vaterland! Let him, if he wants to but without me!'

"Now you're talking like a damn fool," Karl butted in, "Don't you remember what Kurt said? We're staying as long as it's convenient for us."

"Shut up, both of you! Listen to me! Here's what I think. This lieutenant seems to be a novice, alright. But what he says makes a lot of sense to me. No matter how we look at it, we must get food somehow. What's really bugging you, Walter, is the raid tonight, and the risks involved. Isn't it?'

"You damn bet it is!" he growled.

"Well," I continued, "Do you know of a better way to fill your belly?"

"No, I don't! But why don't we wave goodbye to the lieutenant and do it ourselves? Otherwise we'll have to play Robin Hood every night. A party like this is an open invitation to the Russians. They'll hunt us down like rabbits!"

Walter snorted, folded his arms together and leaned against a tree, smugly challenging us.

Karl said, "He has really got a head on his shoulders. If our situation wasn't quite so serious, I'd applaud that speech. Just like a lawyer!"

Walter scowled in reply; inwardly, I had to agree with him, what he said made sense.

"Listen, you guys," I said, "We'll go tonight, and see how things develop. One way or another, we've got to eat — right?"

After further debate, we reached a temporary agreement.

"Let's hurry and gather up our sack before anyone gets suspicious." I warned.

We quickly gathered up the twigs, and returning to our group, we set our quarters in order and hit the hay.

I was awakened by the sound of Unteroffizier Schwarz's voice, "Quickly! Get ready to march!" The blankets were quickly rolled up, guns and munitions gathered. We hurried up to "out marching" position.

The sun had just set, its parting rays gave the scene a ghostly quality. All of the groups met in the middle of the camp site where the lieutenant gave final instructions.

The command to march was given and the column moved. After a few minutes, I was relieved to find that my blood was not frozen in my veins and was circulating freely again. I immediately felt hungry, which goes to prove the saying, "One wish follows another." The choicest dishes of my mother's cuisine, goosestepped in pictures before my eyes, causing me unbearable mental torture. Only with the greatest strength of will could I put aside these tormenting images. My thoughts became anxious as they wandered back to my parents' home, to my wife, to Berlin. I had not been there for two years.

In 1943 I had had a three-week furlough. Of this, seventeen days, were spent hiding from air raids in a cellar. Apprehension crossed my mind as I thought of my wife; she had convinced me to marry her when I was home on furlough. I had pleaded with her to wait until the war was over, but I was unable to change her mind. And so she became a war bride.

A shock woke me from my reveries. The column halted so suddenly that I slammed into Walter, who stood in front of me. I almost knocked him down, and he yelled.

"Watch it, Kurt. You almost gave me a concussion!"

Attention! Group Meier to the front! Advance

patrol. The group moved past us. Pauses were always welcome, although after each rest it took an eternity before our joints were limber enough to pick up the march.

I was diverted for short periods, but my mind began wandering again. Later I became so exhausted it was too much trouble to dream. A few times, I was rudely awakened by tree branches snapping back into my face. Godamn that clumsy Walter! They were painful and made me mad; I swore I would get even with him soon. That opportunity came faster than I expected.

Suddenly, the order was given to halt, and, sure, enough, I slammed into Walter again. He swore at me, but orders came immediately that all group leaders were to go to the front. We worked our way forward to the lieutenant who stood at the edge of the wood. He briefed us thoroughly on your target,

"Men, as you can see, nearby is a settlement. I figure it must be the village of Klein-Doren. It is sparsely populated and spread out. However, the weather is rather unfavorable tonight, much too bright. So we must be particularly cautious, and don't forget those damned dogs! If something goes wrong, and you are detected, then leave at once. Don't engage in gunfire and return immediately to the wood. Unteroffizier Schwarz will lead the raid. Groups Hennig and Klein will remain behind and serve as lateral guards. Are there any questions?"

"I have one," said Unteroffizier Schwarz, "If we are attacked and there are casualties, what are your orders?"

The lieutenant did not answer at once, appearing to struggle with a difficult decision.

"It is entirely up to you, Schwarz. I have to rely on your judgment."

I shuddered when I heard this. The lieutenant was obviously not that inexperienced! He had given a good answer for sure. Such things were unknown in our company, where the wounded were cared for. Of course, there were times when nothing could be done for the critically wounded, but each one of us felt before an encounter, that every human effort would be made to aid us. This gave us the courage to fight. The present circumstances, however, were not normal, and it was not possible to give proper care to the sick and wounded. We all had to look after our own skins. The end of the war was near, but there were still many who would die, up until the last day, hour, even minute of the war.

The sortie was ready to push off and when I gave Walter a machine pistol, he said,

"Damn it ! I'd much rather have my MG; I don't trust these little toys."

Schwarz gave the command to move on, and as soon as we left the woods, the various groups spread out, taking up their positions. The village lay directly to the right of us. Everything was quiet, except occasionally we saw a village dog walking back and forth, yapping. However, there was no sign of the Russians so we moved on.

Now we were only a stone's throw from our destination, and strained our senses to the utmost, but could detect no sound. The two side groups spread out, while Schwarz's group crept forward. We reached a fence.

The silence was excruciating, any minute we expected the barking of some watchdog. It didn't come, which was a good sign. We slipped through the gate door, and hid behind a pile of wood. In the darkness I could make out a feeble light. Two men remained behind the wood pile, while the rest of us crept forward to safety near the side of the barn.

Before us was the backyard of a house, the rear entrance facing us. I looked around feverishly to see indications of a doghouse, but greatly relieved, I concluded there was none.

Schwarz gave the signal to approach, and in a few short spurts, we reached the building. Hearts beating fast, we threw ourselves against the wall, while two soldiers stationed themselves on each side of the door. Three of us covered them, our trigger fingers ready. Schwarz knocked against the door, and he was answered by loud barking! My God, I thought, that bitch will give us all away! From inside we heard a man's voice quieting the dog.

"Who's there?"

"German soldiers. Please open the door."

It was opened half way.

"Come in quickly."

When we were all in, the door was shut firmly behind us.

"Just a minute while I tie up the dog."

The man returned soon afterwards and we moved into the light, and for the first time, I saw the face of our host. He was old with short, white hair and a large, bulbous nose set squarely in his wrinkled face. He asked, in a deep voice, "What do you want?"

Schwarz quickly explained the purpose of our mission. His next question was, "How many are you?"

"Sixty-two."

"Impossible. I have barely enough for my own family. The Russians carted off everything that was not nailed down. All I can give you is some bread, wurst, and cheese."

The old man went to a door, and opening it, called two women. Momentarily, a young one and an old one appeared. Whispering, he instructed them to gather up some provisions. After they had gone, he turned back to us, saying,

"Should the Russians discover you were here, my entire family could be shot."

Schwarz had no comment on this, but instead asked thoughtfully,

"Do you know where they are?"

"Everywhere, mein Herr!"

For emphasis, he made a wide circle with his arm. My God, I thought, we'll never reach our lines! As soon as the women returned with food, which we concealed in our blankets, we hurried out the door. The old man warned us,

"Hurry up. The Russians often come here late at night looking for German soldiers."

"One more question," Schwarz asked, "How many Russian soldiers are here in the village?"

"Hard to say; they come and go. I would estimate that two companies are stationed here all the time."

He closed the door behind us and we raced back to our anxious comrades at the wood pile. Then we retreated back to the woods with lightning speed. The protection of the trees felt good at this moment.

Most of us thought we would now have something to eat for our efforts, but we were sorely disappointed. The lieutenant put Schwarz in charge of provisions. Then he called the spearhead together, immediately giving the command to move on. Naturally, there was dissension, and Walter came over to me and raised a ruckus.

"What do you say now? Are you satisfied? I tell you, it's time to cut out!"

We had no time to talk, because we had to march at a fast pace. For over an hour, we raced under the trees, while the night seemed endless. At first, I cursed Walter for the damn twigs and branches which he snapped back carelessly into my face; later, however, even swearing became too much of a strain. Hunger and exhaustion had made me irritable, and I was in an angry mood.

After what seemed an eternity, we pulled up to the edge of an open field. The lieutenant called a halt.

"Men, we are going to rest here for the day. The dawn will come in perhaps an hour, and each group will find a place to sleep. Take good cover against reconnaissance aircraft. And one more thing, I did not issue the rations before, as it was too dangerous for our undertaking to stay where we were. That is all. Start moving!"

Walter, Karl and I found a suitable spot, and as soon as we had gathered underbrush for our sack, we sank down, exhausted.

"Kurt, wake up!"

I heard a voice from afar calling my name. Someone was shaking me roughly, and I woke up; it was already broad daylight.

"Come on," Schwarz was saying to me, "Chow time!"

At last I felt my limbs functioning again. When we approached the lieutenant, the food had already been divided into portions. The rations were small but they looked mighty good. Each of us was given a piece of bread, wurst and cheese; just enough for a teaser.

"Schwarz!"

"Herr Lieutenant!"

"Your group will relieve the sentries. See that they have enough time to eat; then have them take their positions."

"Jawohl, Herr Lieutenant!"

Ravenously, we attacked our rations. Schwarz advised us not to eat all of it, but to save some for later.

"Leave a little for tonight, men. We don't know when we'll have another opportunity to eat."

Walter's retort was immediate,

"What I have in my stomach now, no one can take away."

Such was Walter's philosophy for as long as I had known him. In Finland we were given rations for two days, but they never lasted for more than one. On the second day, we just went hungry. Walter used to justify his actions by pointing to the label on the cans, explaining,

"It says, 'For immediate consumption'!"

After our repast, we went off to relieve the guard.

A few days later, the food situation turned from bad to worse. Morale and discipline had gone to hell, and there was scarcely a man who could master his hunger or the grueling ordeal of continuous marching. So far, we had attempted two raids. The first time we were shot at and the second time we were chased away by dog's barking. It was sheer luck that we found a deserted silo with some potatoes remaining from the harvest. For two days we had lived on them, half roasted and half raw. The snow was melting now and that impeded our progress enormously. Marching was unbearable as the land became marshy. We sank into the mud, and water ran through our torn boots. It was like walking through a swamp. This ordeal completely sapped what was left of our energy.

The soldier's discipline which had been instilled in us for years had disappeared. There was open dissension as the voices of mutiny were heard. My two buddies tried to convince me to desert. I was tempted, but I was afraid — what would happen if we ran into the Russians? They didn't need guns; they could kill us with clubs!

As it happened, luck was still with us. That night we came upon a farm, whose owner was an old World War I veteran. He proved himself a hero and a patriot of the first caliber. His two sons were soldiers, somewhere in Russia, and he offered his help immediately,

"I hope my sons will receive the same help when they need it."

His name was Lebermann, and he said the Russians did not come around too often looking for German soldiers. He asked us into his barn, saying,

"Don't worry. I'll keep an eye out for you. Many years ago I wore the same uniform. I want to ask only one thing of you. Please leave by dawn."

We asked him the distance to the Baltic Sea.

"Approximately thirty kilometers."

Soon, he and his wife went into the house to prepare some food for us. He asked for two men to carry the milk. We posted four guards, as usual, for the night, and didn't need an anesthetic to make us fall asleep.

Unfortunately, the night was too short, but Lebermann's shouting soon brought us to reality. To our surprise, he had prepared a milk soup, which we greatly appreciated. His concern, and courage were remarkable.

He was a real hero and before we thanked him and said good-bye, he gave us a few instructions for our safety. He refused to accept any thanks, but asked God for our speedy return to our loved ones. My throat was choked up and we were all deeply touched. Most of us clapped him on the shoulder. Battle-scarred though we were, our emotions got the best of us.

During the day, we stayed in the depths of the forest while scouts were sent out to reconnoiter the area. They returned with several men, (including an unteroffizier who had been separated from his unit) who were wandering around lost. They were very happy to see us though they were in the same poor condition. One private had a dirty bandage covered with dry blood around his head. His face was waxen and his eyes deeply feverish. Unteroffizier Pawellek reported to the lieutenant, explaining what had happened to his troop.

Three days ago they were still a full platoon. Spurred on by hunger, they raided a village about thirty kilometers away. Apparently the time was poorly chosen because they were discovered and shots exchanged. Two Russians were killed, while three Germans were left for dead in the dirty snow. The private had received a head wound. The raiding party was chased in all directions by the Russians, and he didn't know what had happened to the others.

Lieutenant Sommer brooded and kept silent as he regarded the wounded soldier. Without turning his head, he barked out the name of a medic whom he ordered to attend to the wounded man in the best way possible. He had apparently made a decision, because he turned to us, smiling helplessly,

"Men, our family is getting larger, and with it more responsibilities. We are approximately thirty kilometers from the shoreline of the Baltic, and if everything goes well, we should be able to reach our destination in two nights. What we can expect when we arrive there, is uncertain, but I hope we'll be able to catch a ship which will take us to safety and freedom. Because we are not very far from Kolberg, I expect a higher concentration of Russian troops ahead. We must, therefore, double our caution and at any cost avoid engagements with them. Look after the wounded private; his weapon is to be given to Walter . . . what's the name of that private?"

"Novak, Herr Lieutenant!"

"Right."

After Walter took the gun, we discussed our new situation.

"You know, Kurt," he said, "So far, we've had pretty good luck. But those poor buggers who just joined us, really got it. That could have happened to us."

Karl said, 'I'm not superstitious, but I think we should remain with this group."

I agreed.

"The lieutenant isn't doing too badly after all. Maybe he is lucky. Let's stay!"

"That doesn't leave me much choice," Walter said, "I have to look after you guys."

With that, he turned his back to us, and rolled himself into his blanket, as casually as if he hadn't a care in the world. Karl and I smoked another cigarette, then we followed suit.

I couldn't sleep. My thoughts wandered back to Finland again — it was October, 1944. Finland had capitulated. We were in retreat, and the Russian offensive was out to destroy us completely. During one barrage, a mortar shell hit too close and I was wounded. At first there was a terrible pain in my shoulder; then my knee felt as if it had been torn off. I nearly fainted from the pain. There was no cover anywhere and I was pinned down by heavy mortar fire. Then I saw Walter who sprinted over to aid me. I will never forget the first thing he said,

"I can't leave you alone for a minute, can I?"

Fortunately, my wound was not as bad as it appeared at first. The knee was still there, swollen to twice its normal size. Later the sliver in my shoulder was removed in an operation. When I rejoined my company afterwards in Norway, I tried to express my appreciation for the bravery Walter had shown on the battlefield, but he did not give me a chance.

"Shut up!" he said, "You'd have done the same for me, and you know it! Let's get drunk and forget about it."

Even remembering the past could not completely obliterate the present. Somehow, now, we must get to the sea. By nightfall, we were ready to continue the march. Unteroffizier Pawellek was appointed our group leader and Unteroffizier Schwarz was made second in command to Sommer. We made good progress without encountering any impediments. Shortly after midnight we came upon a village, and like hungry beasts, searched until we found an isolated farm house. We considered it ideal for our purposes, but our luck abandoned us this time.

The farmer flatly refused to lend any assistance in our flight for freedom, and with great audacity, he threatened to warn the Russians. Infuriated and cursing like a mad man, Walter leveled his gun to firing position, intending to pump the traitor full of lead. Instantly, the Lieutenant shoved the gun barrel into the air.

"Don't be a damn fool!" he exploded, "Do you want the whole Russian army here? Leave this dog to grovel and let's get the hell out of here!"

The tenseness of the moment was felt by many of the men who agreed with Walter. But the Lieutenant's wisdom prevailed, and driven by necessity, we hastily grabbed what we could find — some cucumbers, carrots and a few potatoes; then disappeared into the relative safety of the forest.

After marching several hours, the two advance scouts suddenly signalled halt — they had bad news. Reporting to Lieutenant Sommer, they explained that directly ahead, a highway crossed our path. But that was not all — the highway was covered with Russian trucks that were not moving; something was blocking the traffic.

The Lieutenant growled, *"Scheissdreck!"* (Shit!)

Then he called for the group leaders. After some discussion, they went off to investigate the matter personally. Upon returning, they called us all together. The Lieutenant explained that the highway lay directly across our path, and somehow we had to cross it.

"Men!" he added, "Nothing is going to stop us from reaching the Baltic Sea, now that we've come so far! We will plow our way across that street with bullets, and before those damn Russians know what hit them, we'll be swallowed up by the forest and the darkness!"

Walter rammed his elbow into my back.

"What did I tell you?"

I had my own ideas about this brilliant plan too, but I kept quiet. The lieutenant continued,

"We can't stay here any longer! By dawn we must be far away and under cover!"

He was a real smart aleck; without giving us time to disagree or think for ourselves, he ordered us to take up positions immediately. All I had time for was to urge Karl and Walter to stay close to me so we would not lose each other.

We captured the street in a manner that reminded me of past glory. The following day, however, we paid dearly for this act of grandeur. The Russians pursued us with everything they had: horses, dogs, and at least two companies of men. They pursued us from one forest to another, and several of our men lost their lives during the chase; others disappeared and we never saw them again.

We ran in all directions. Everybody fled for his life. I fell down several times and splashed in the mud. So did Walter and Karl. Somehow though, we found the gumption to get up again. Perhaps the help and mutual encouragement we gave each other did it. Towards nightfall the Russians stopped their pursuit; more dead than alive, we slumped to the forest floor. Exhausted, we just did not give a damn; an attitude which left us on the ground for several hours.

Later, when the count was made, 26 men were either dead of missing; among these were Unteroffiziers Schwarz and Pawellek. The lieutenant appointed me leader for the third group. That was all I needed now!

Somehow the lieutenant managed to get us moving a few hours after dark, and we pushed on. That night we got nothing to eat; for nourishment we could chew on our dirty fingernails.

Towards four a.m. we stepped out of the forest, onto the sands of the Baltic Sea. Glorious God, we had made it! A powerful emotion gripped our hearts and pride in our accomplishment was stronger than our hunger or fatigue. We stood mute before the most beautiful sight in the world; the ugly, green, restless waters of the Baltic. A brisk wind came in from the sea, and we had never breathed anything sweeter in our lives. All our petty grievances were laid aside — out there was FREEDOM!

The lieutenant's voice brought us back to reality.

"We've made it!" he said, and I detected a note of pride in his voice.

"But we are not free from danger yet!"

As if to compensate for our moment of weakness, he issued orders in rapid succession. Sentries were posted to guard our present position and my group was ordered to scout the beach to our left. I instructed my men to walk at an arm's distance. Walter and I took the lead, while Karl was the rear guard. After some walking, during which time we encountered nothing suspicious, we came to a place where the beach twisted in the shape of a horseshoe. Walter sniffed in the air in his own inimitable manner. I did not like the scenery either, and gave the signal to halt.

I did not trust my eyes at first, but, out in the bay, was a large boat! I looked again — no doubt about it!

There was not a living soul in the area and I grabbed Walter's arm, excitedly, speaking in his ear.

"Do you see it out there?"

Walter nodded.

"What do you think?"

The wind blew his words away. We kept our positions, but did not see anything suspicious, and I gave the signal to pull back.

When we returned I reported to Lieutenant Sommer. He became disturbed and after walking on the beach for awhile, he asked for two men who knew something about boats. After they volunteered, he outlined a plan.

They were instructed to find out if the craft was seaworthy. We broke camp and took up positions from where I located the boat first. It was almost too quiet.

"Unteroffizier Hennig!"

"Herr Lieutenant!"

"Your group will go with the two men and guard them!"

"Jawohl, Herr Lieutenant!"

Before leaving, the lieutenant grabbed his arm, and said, solicitously,

"Be careful, man!"

Along the protective edge of the trees, Hennig's men worked their way to the bay where they took up positions. The two men descended into the icy sea. When the water reached their chests, they hoisted themselves into the boat. We followed them with our eyes, keeping our fingers crossed. The lieutenant moved from one place to another, restless because of tension. After they had completed their investigation, the two men returned to the beach.

Now the lieutenant made his biggest mistake. He gave the order to approach the others at the far end of the beach, without taking any precautions. We were almost destroyed as soon as we reached the men who tried to give us a report through chattering teeth. It seemed that hell hit us.

Machine gun and rifle fire caught us completely unprepared. Confusion and death was everywhere. Grouped together on the white sands, we were a target that could hardly be missed. Some comrades were dead before hitting the ground, while the rest of us ran towards the trees, away from the firing.

I jumped into the bushes and fell over a root, hitting the ground hard. I lost my weapon and lay half-conscious on the ground. I thought I had broken every bone in my body, and I lay there completely out of breath, waiting to die. If only someone would be merciful enough to finish me off!

But, as had happened so often before, I picked up the pieces and continued. Animation returned slowly, and I crawled on all fours, got up, and stumbled. I could not find my weapon! I listened to the noise around me, expecting to be caught any minute. When I began to think clearly, my first question was, "Where are Walter and Karl and the others?"

I managed to hobble a short distance then my legs gave out. The noise faded into the distance while a voice inside me kept saying, "Don't stop! Keep going!" I did not dare to rest. Throwing away the full magazines from my sub-machine gun, I moved somewhat easier through the underbrush. By sheer luck, I must have headed in the right direction, because far to the right, I could still hear shouting as well as shooting.

A little longer, I thought. I must find a place to crawl into and hide. With my very last reserves, I pursued the same direction and then, like an animal who knows the end is coming, I crawled under a thick bush and curled up. The battery was dead. Sleep was what I most wished for.

How long I dozed, I have no idea but I was still alive and undetected. I strained listening but heard no sound. Twilight was setting about me; the sun was down, but it was not yet completely dark. Where to now? I must find a village where I could get food to regain my strength. Otherwise, I would not last much longer.

In the meantime darkness descended and everything seemed hopeless. The wood was endless, and I was at the end of my strength. Many times, I felt overpowered by the stillness, darkness, and the mighty depths of the forest. I was tempted to cry out for my lost buddies, Walter and Karl.

Suddenly, I heard a noise; I listened, carefully, but it disappeared. I walked further, and in the far distance, I discerned some activity. As I continued it became more pronounced and as I began to distinguish motor noises, my hopes soared. But it was still an eternity before I left the woods and emerged into an open field.

CHAPTER TWO

I knew that a village must be nearby, and I cut across the fields. I was correct, a village lay only a few hundred yards away.

I looked it over for a while and it did not appear to be dangerous, so I crept cautiously towards an isolated house until I was only a few feet from it. Everything was quiet and I was particularly grateful that there were no howling dogs about to sound the alarm.

With great caution, I crept to the window. Inside, I heard voices but could not understand them. Then, I thought I heard a child's voice. I knocked on the window; the talking stopped immediately. I knocked again; then I crept to the door. From within came the sound of a woman's voice.

"Who is there?"

"Relax," I said. "A German soldier."

The door was partly opened, and someone grabbed my arm, dragging me in. Immediately, the door was shut and a beam drawn across it.

I regarded my new surroundings, though the light was dim and it took awhile for me to adjust to the semi-darkness. To my astonishment, I found myself in a large living room with many women and several children. I did not see any men.

I sensed there was no immediate danger here. Everyone stared at me, and the children, with wide open eyes, ran to their mothers for protection.

My questions were fired like pistol shots.

"Are there any Russians here? Where is the front? Can you give me something to eat?"

As I looked around, a young woman with a sympathetic face and sad eyes, spoke to me,

"One question at a time, soldier. First, the front is far away from here and advancing daily, and Russians are in the villages guarding all the streets. They often search the houses for German soldiers, and when they don't find any, German girls and women are welcome substitutes. Their screams can be heard for miles. That is why we're all together in this house; we give each other courage and there is some safety here. Until now, we have been lucky, and have been unmolested, God be thanked."

I was unable to speak, and she continued,

"Naturally, we have something for you to eat. What's your name, soldier?"

"Kurt Stock."

"Magda Behrens is my name." She shook hands, trying to smile.

"Kurt, why are you alone?"

In short sentences, I described our unsuccessful attempt. Magda shook her head, sympathetically.

"What do you intend to do now?"

I shrugged my shoulders. She commented,

"The war is coming to an end. Why don't you change into a civilian and wait it out? You can find work on any farm around here, help is needed desperately."

I looked at her in astonishment. Without waiting for an answer, she continued,

"You have done your duty and what is happening now is only mass murder. Be sensible and try to save your skin."

"But I have no civilian clothing."

"Don't worry about it. We'll find some. In the meantime, you can wash up."

Magda led me into the kitchen. In a short time she had gotten some toilet things together, even providing a razor. When she left the kitchen, I removed my uniform and washed myself thoroughly. As I leaned over the mirror, I recoiled in horror. Was the gaunt face with the weary, hunted eyes mine? Now I understood why the children had run to their mothers and why the women had trembled — I looked like a caveman! When I finished shaving, I did look more human.

Magda soon returned with an armload of things, putting them on the table. She looked me over critically, saying,

"You look much better now. Put these things on while I burn your uniform in the stove."

She put my dogtag, compass, *soldbuch* (I.D. card), medals, and letters in a container saying she'd bury it in the garden and I could have the things back when the war was over.

The civilian clothes fit fairly well, and I felt more comfortable now. When Magda returned to the kitchen, she seemed pleased with my appearance. My heart went out to this good woman, who had rescued me from the wilderness. We did not discuss the consequences to her and the others if the Russians discovered I had been there. After I had eaten, I thanked her, saying I would leave immediately.

She thought for a moment, then said,

"Don't worry about that now, I'm returning to the others to see what we can do for you."

Magda hesitated, thinking. To this day, I haven't forgotten the meal she served me. I had been plucked from danger and death to feminine warmth and safety, however temporary.

I wondered why she was doing this for me, concluding that she would reveal it in her own good time.

Magda left me in the kitchen but returned shortly with good news. She had talked to the others who agreed to hide me over night.

"Now listen carefully. Should a patrol come searching for German soldiers, we've a good hiding place for you. However, you must stay there and not move, even if you hear screams and shouting, you must not budge from there until I say so. Tomorrow morning I will send you to Frau Arnheim who is a short distance away. Her husband died a year ago, and she needs help on her farm badly."

She searched my face for the answer. I thought it over again, considering my own safety. Where else could I go? I had no choice, and she was glad to hear that I accepted her hospitality.

When we returned to the others in the living room, she pointed to a couch, saying, "Here is your bed." I thanked everyone for their kindness, excused myself and turned in to sleep.

But sleep eluded me. My face burned because the room was overheated. With everyone together in the room, it was very stuffy, and I tossed from side to side. I lay awake for hours while all sorts of thoughts crossed my mind, driving sleep away. Finally my nerves quieted down and from faraway I heard a child's voice, then I fell asleep before I could hear the answer.

Many times during the night, I awakened, listening. No patrols came by but in my nightmares, I saw them everywhere.

I dreamed that I fought single-handedly against an entire company. I fired and kept on shooting until I ran out of ammunition, but no one fell. A thousand hands grabbed me! I woke up soaking wet, relieved to find it was just a dream.

After that, many Russian tanks pursued me and I zig-zagged like a rabbit until I came to the Baltic. "Prison!" I thought. Behind me were the tanks and Russian soldiers — laughing — until I awakened with my hands pressed to my ears, sitting up on the couch.

It was early morning, and wearily, I looked around the room. People slept on the floor in various positions. A few small children were crawling around; a baby cried, but quieted when he received his mother's breast. Carrying my torn shoes, I tip-toed carefully over the sleeping figures, going into the kitchen.

Magda was already up and busy over the stove. I greeted her, and washed the cold sweat from my hands and face.

Magda fried me an egg and gave me some bread and coffee. To me it was a banquet.

"How did you sleep?" Magda asked.

"Terrible. Ivan was after me all night. How about you?"

"I didn't sleep well either."

We looked at each other across the table. I saw fear and sadness in Magda's eyes. I felt as if I had known her a long time although really, we were almost strangers. The night before I had been lost and terrified and her warmth had made me feel like a human being again. We were two of a kind; both hunted.

My eyes caught the strong, well shaped fingers, and

on her right hand was a wedding ring. Before I could ask about it, she broke the silence:

"My husband died in the Caucasus."

I felt like a captured thief, and said something by way of apology, trying to find words of sympathy.

She changed the subject immediately,

"You'd better be going," she advised. "I'll see if the coast is clear."

She stood up, put on her coat, and disappeared through the door. Soon she returned, saying.

"It's alright."

When I left, I tried to thank her, but she would not hear of it. Her parting words were,

"Take care and be strong."

After one more look, and shaking hands, I disappeared down the street. It was empty so early in the morning and a cold wind blew me along. I pulled my cap down over my face, and rolled my overcoat collar over my neck, and started towards the farmhouse. As luck would have it, Magda and I never saw each other again.

Luckily for me, the streets were deserted. However, I came across a farmer in a cart who rode past me without paying any attention. Following Magda's instructions I turned off the highway after a short distance into a side road leading to the Arnheim farm. Soon I reached a fence and ahead was the barn and the master's house.

The weather was fair and I walked quickly. A dog ran to the fence and welcomed me with barking. Since he was wagging his tail, I assumed he was not dangerous and I quieted him by talking to him gently. Together we walked the rest of the distance to the house.

A woman stood in the doorway looking at us. She shouted for the dog to quiet down.

"*Guten morgen, mein Herr!*"

"*Guten morgen!* I would like to speak to Frau Arnheim."

"Just a moment, I'll call her. She's my sister."

A woman in her forties came to the door. We exchanged greetings and I explained why I had come. She regarded me suspiciously, so I mentioned that Magda Behrens had sent me. This brought about a change in her attitude, and she invited me into the house.

She asked me dozens of questions but I was discreet, telling her as much as I thought she should know. Finally she said,

"Mr. Stock, I really do need a helper around the farm. But tell me what will happen if the Russians find that I am keeping a German soldier in disguise. The consequences could be terrible for all of us."

She shrugged her shoulders. I pleaded with her.

"Please listen to me, Frau Arnheim! The Russians won't be able to find out! I have no identification with me, and we can trust Magda and the others not to give me away. Also, I'm completely unknown here."

She sat there, still undecided; I begged further,

"Frau Arnheim, where can I go? I don't know a soul! How am I going to eat?"

"Well!", she said finally, "Let's try it. Perhaps God has sent us a sign."

She called her sister back and introduced us. Her name was Trudy.

"Trudy, Herr Stock is a refugee who is going to work for us."

She did not tell her sister the truth. She asked if I had breakfast, and when I nodded, she said,

"Come on, then. I'll show you where to start."

We entered the barn, and she pointed to the pig pen,

"This needs to be cleaned, first."

She gave me some tools, and I went to work. I made good progress in spite of the pigs. When I was almost finished, Frau Arnheim called me to lunch.

As I walked towards the house, I froze in my tracks. A Russian cavalry patrol had just turned into the yard.

My heart almost jumped out of my throat. Panicky, I thought, "Don't show them you're scared!"

They watered their horses and I noticed one man regarded me strangely. A few soldiers entered the house, while I moved slowly towards the wood pile, acting as if I were wood chopping. In the meantime the idiotic dog barked its head off!

The Russians now left the house, carrying apples in their hands. Laughingly they had some fun pitching apples at the dog. They doubled over with laughter, but the one with his own suspicions came over to me. My feelings cannot be exactly described, but I thought — "I've had it!" It was the first time I faced a Russian without a weapon in my hand.

He came toward me pointing his rifle at chest level. His Asiatic eyes ran through me,

"Soldat-Ja?"

Fear prickled my spine, and I shook my head like a deaf and dumb mute! Daring not to reveal my fear, I feigned great interest in silencing the dog. I began cursing him, and with deliberation I bent warily down to pick up a stick to strike him with. The ruse worked! The Russian shook his head and joined the others. The order was given to mount, and in a few minutes they were out of sight. I never again experienced such fear.

As I walked unsteadily into the house, I had the feeling that my knees were made of rubber. When I had finished eating, I was given the bad news.

Frau Arnheim's face was bathed in tears as she explained that the Russians had ordered her to leave the farm within a day. The entire village was being evacuated; she continued to sob incessantly. Her sister tried to comfort her, without success. Frau Arnheim blurted out,

"My God! How long will this hideous war continue!"

It had been very difficult for Frau Arnheim since her husband died a year ago. Somehow, she managed with very little help, to run the farm by herself. I tried to find words to comfort her, but they were hard in coming. After all, my future was grim, too.

However, I offered to help her. With eyes full of tears, she thanked me, gratefully accepting my offer. She explained that days ago the Russians had taken one of the horses, and there was only one remaining.

"I'll pack our belongings in a wagon, and move in wiht my uncle at the village."

I was instructed to dig a hole in the southeast corner of the barn, where I helped bury her valuables. I was surprised to find they were worth a small fortune. When I had covered everything over with earth, Frau Arnheim came out with a pack of cigarettes and put them in my shirt. It was very thoughtful of her to show such consideration at a time like this.

As we were ready to leave, I noticed a pain in my chest and felt my temperature rising; a new cause for concern. Before we left, we opened the doors to the stalls and barns, letting the animals out.

The wagon was piled high with ustensils, bedding, clothing and assorted goods. It was hard for her to part with many items which held memories and I had to convince her to leave many things behind.

I held the reins to our solitary horse as we journeyed off into the unknown. Even Nero, the dog, was subdued, walking silently beside the wagon, his head bowed to the ground.

We did not speak for a while, but I suspected what Frau Arnheim was thinking; I sensed that she was too embarrassed to mention the subject, so I broached it to her,

"You know, Frau Arnheim?" I said, "Perhaps it's time for me to make it on my own."

"Well, Herr Stock", she said, evidently relieved that I was independent, "As you can see, I am no longer in the position to employ you now. Of course, you are welcome to accompany me to my uncle's, but I don't think the situation will be any brighter there. I'm grateful for the help you've given me already, and I will let you decide."

"Listen," I said with a sudden flash of inspiration, "Why don't you give me one of your shovels, and I'll fade into the wagon train as if I was a farm hand."

She nodded her head. I took the shovel and said good-bye. After shaking hands, I jumped off the wagon and walked ahead quickly without looking back.

Wiederum verlassen und verstossen.

Once again abandoned and cast out.

I soon caught up with a heavily laden wagon, and followed a short distance behind it, my shovel balanced loosely on my shoulder. No one paid any attention, and after going along for a distance, the wagon turned off to the left of the road following a field. I was undecided whether to follow it, and I even played with the idea of going back to see Magda, but dismissed it from my mind because I would be endangering them; besides, I was beginning to feel fatigued and the symptoms of illness returned.

But as I walked, I came in view of a lonely farm. No one was in sight; to all appearances it was deserted. I decided to investigate.

I entered the large farm house and there wasn't a soul in sight! That was fine with me, though I almost collapsed right where I stood. But I had to make sure, so I pulled myself together to explore the upper floor. In the attic I could detect nothing but old furniture and boxes. What an ideal place to hide, I thought! That same moment, my strained ears caught a sound. Every muscle in my tired body was alerted, as I tried to hear better. Then I heard something again! It seemed to come from the left wall where a drop curtain hung. My first impulse was to leave without investigating further, but something impelled me to pull aside the curtain. Behind it was a door. Slowly I turned the knob, opening it. A woman stood before me. Stifling a scream and staring at me with terrified eyes. It was a mutual shock; I stood riveted to the floor.

When I recovered a little, I saw that the door concealed an apartment. The woman had been cooking a meal when I arrived.

She spoke first. "Thank heaven! I was sure you were a Russian soldier."

My answer was to shake my head stupidly in denial. "No, I'm not," I managed.

Without noticing it, we both spoke in a broad Berlin dialect. Upon realizing this, we both began laughing nervously.

"Well, why don't you come in, Mr. ...?"

"Kurt Stock:"

"Good. My name is Frieda Wagner, and these are my two children."

She pointed to two shy children climbing to her skirt.

"Their names are Helga and Christa."

She asked me to sit down, curious to know what brought me there.

"It's a long story and ..." I began.

"Excuse me, I think some sort of precautions should be taken."

Helga was instructed to go downstairs and lock the door, and then return upstairs to act as lookout at the one window which gave light to the attic.

Christa, the younger girl, with a doll's face and long braids, asked, "Please Mommy. Give me something to do!"

"Certainly, Christa. Follow Helga and make sure that she is alert. If someone approaches, I want you to come right away and tell me. Now hurry up, you two!"

Frieda turned back to me, sighing.

"I worry so much about them. What a shame they must stand guard instead of going to school or playing."

"Do the Russians know you are here?"

"Yes, but they don't bother me. I occasionally do domestic work for them. For the time being, I am not afraid."

We talked casually — it was like a visit home. I asked her about Berlin, and we discussed places that we knew, personal friends, and the war. We learned that we came from the same section of Berlin, within walking distance of one another. She described the air raid in which her husband had been killed, and how she was later evacuated to Pomerania.

Then I asked her, "Where is the owner of the farm?"

"Ah! He ran off the day the Russians came to the village, leaving me here to fend for myself."

She shed a few tears.

"Forgive me. Everything has been bottled up inside me, and I can't show the children that I am worried or afraid. But talking to you made me unable to restrain myself any more."

"As the saying goes, when the heart is full, the mouth speaks." I said. Immediately I broke into a coughing fit, as if I would never stop. My head was aching and the pain in my chest had become unbearable. Now it was Frieda's turn to look concerned. She felt my forehead with her hand.

"My God, you've really caught something, Kurt. You've got a high fever!"

She ran to a cabinet, returning with aspirins. After a little while I felt better but nevertheless I began shaking with severe chills.

"You'd better go to bed!" she told me emphatically. I tried not to face the fact that I was seriously ill but I was unable to avoid it. Under her commanding eyes, I plodded towards the bed and collapsed.

What happened from then on, I learned from Frieda. For about a week I grew worse. She told me later that I reached a point at which she could only pray for me.

I was delirious with pneumonia, recognizing nothing, not even her. That I survived, must be attributed to the selfless care that Frieda, my guardian angel, gave me during this crisis. She forced chicken broth through my feverish lips and prayed for hours at my bedside. Indeed, that I am alive today is due to the loving kindness and care of many good women, who rescued me from a state lower than a dog's.

The two girls also behaved marvellously during my illness, taking turns in doing guard duty and worrying as much as Frieda did about my condition.

But at last the crisis was over and I was able to recognize my surroundings, and sit up in bed. Fortunately, there was no food shortage. The farmer had been a Nazi party member and had fled before the Russians came. Before he left he turned all the stock loose. Cows, chickens, geese and pigs roamed about the property. We had all the eggs and milk we could use.

A few day after I recovered from my delirium, I was still very weak but could move about and sit at the table for meals. I think it was around March 24th, as I sat in the kitchen waiting for breakfast that the door opened and Christa ran in shouting,

"Mother! Two Russian soldiers are coming!"

"Quickly, Kurt! To your hiding place!"

As soon as I was concealed, she ran down to meet them. The sound of soldiers' boots reverberated through the house and I could hear voices, but couldn't make out what they were saying.

Frieda left with them and Helga released me. We watched together from the attic window. Hours passed, and still no sign of Frieda. I was becoming very concerned. Finally, I saw her running up the field road towards the house. I knew immediately that something was wrong. I met her at the front door and she threw herself on my chest, crying hysterically.

She had been raped by three Russian soldiers while

they held her at gun point. When I heard this, I felt I could no longer endure the cruelty and violence of this war. But what could I do? I was still weak and sick, and could only clench my teeth together in frustration and despair.

Nothing I said could comfort her; at most, I cautioned her to show restraint before the children. Helga was anxious to know what had happened and Frieda said she had bruised her shinbone against the step as she ran and it was very painful.

CHAPTER THREE

The next day, we saw troop transports going down the road. Soldiers and vehicles were crowded together for miles. No one disturbed us, however. We later learned these troops were being released, replaced by others. Besides the Russians, there were now some Polish soldiers in the village.

Two days later, all citizens had to report to the village square immediately. With the order was the suggestion we take only our most essential personal belongings. Frieda and I discussed the situation; there was no use in running any more. Wherever I went, it would be the same; if I didn't give myself up, I probably would be caught, and perhaps shot.

Frieda had a good idea; she suggested we go as a family, reasoning that the new troops were not as well informed as the ones who left, and would accept our story. We loaded up a baby carriage with food and other items, and left.

We arrived in the village around twelve o'clock. I remember the day exactly. It was the day I was captured. It was March 27, 1945. The square was crowded and confused with much anxiety and tension in the air. Russian and Polish soldiers ran about barking orders, forcing people into a line, sometimes with a curse or rifle butt. The interpreters wore white arm-bands, shouting orders right and left. We were pushed into a group outside the Russian headquarters. An officer spoke to us in broken German. ordering us about.

"Women and children — Left! Men — Right!"

He pointed furiously to compensate for his inability to communicate properly. Frieda and I spoke perhaps ten words more, then we were separated. She, too, passed out of my life. When I last saw her, a soldier was prodding her with his rifle to force her to move on.

The men were ordered to a nearby farmhouse where Russian soldiers stood guard with their rifles trained on us. We were led through the gate behind a wire fence where about thirty men stood in small groups. Now I knew that the hunt was over and the quarry brought to bay; I was in prison. In the beginning I was optimistic, but I was not to see the end for many years.

I found out that we were waiting for interrogation, and those who left us did not return. I stayed in a corner away from the door as long as I could, trying to invent a plausible story. It was both good and bad that I had no papers — good, because it could not be proven I was a soldier; bad, because they would distrust anything I said. I reasoned that I'd be safest staying away from the truth. The error of this decision, I learned later on.

I took a closer look at the house now, curious about what happened to the others after the Russians finished their interrogation.

A woman was standing near the fence with a package of sandwiches that she begged me to throw up to her son who was at the upper window.

The window was open and a boyish face with blond hair signalled me to throw the package up to him. After the second try, he was able to secure the sandwiches. Unfortunately, I disregarded the lower window of the interrogation room. A Russian officer inside knocked against the window pane; then he waved his arm towards me. Apparently I must have done something wrong, because he pulled out his pistol and shot at me through the window. The bullet whizzed past my head and in seconds, I was flat on the ground. As no more shots came, I jumped to my feet and ran like a scared rabbit. However, before I could catch my breath, the Russian officer stood in the doorway, singling me out to a guard. He shouted just one word — *Him*, and the soldier pushed me all the way to the interrogation room.

I stood before the desk, and the officer asked me in tolerable German,

"What were you doing before my window?"

After I told him, he grinned and pointed to the hole in the window, saying,

"You almost paid too high a price for a good deed."

Then the interrogation began; when he found out I had no papers, his questions were short and direct.

Name? Place of Birth? Age?

"Soldat?!"

"Yes, until 1943. Then I was discharged for factory production in Berlin."

"You worked in Berlin? Then, what are you doing here in Pomerania?"

He stared at me mercilessly, and I answered without hesitation,

"The factory I worked at was totally destroyed by an air raid and I moved in temporarily with my aunt here in Pomerania."

I could tell by the way he looked at me that he did

not believe my story. He gave a command to an aide, then addressed me,

"Go upstairs to the others."

The guard led me to the upper room where the young man leaned against the wall holding his sandwiches.

He thanked me, adding,

"My God, you sure had some bad luck down there!"

"It wasn't your fault." I said simply.

I found myself a place near the window and dropped to the floor. An old man with blue lips and watery eyes whispered, "I wonder what's in store for us."

Another answered, "Breaking rocks in Siberia!"

"Or a slow death in the salt mines subsisting on bread and water!"

I heard the voice of the teenager near me,

"Comrade, would you like a sandwich?"

I turned my head and gazed into a pair of questioning blue eyes.

"Good sausage." he added.

"Yes — why not? Thanks."

With our backs to the wall, we sat on the floor and munched on sanwiches.

"What's your name?" he asked timidly.

"Kurt. And yours?"

"Peter Dombrowski."

More men were coming upstairs, and soon the room was full. Some had been released, due to poor health, age, or the loss of a limb during battle. I was uneasy, but not afraid; the unknown was nothing new to me as a soldier, merely a hated companion, whom I had learned to deal with.

I dozed off for a while, my thoughts going back to Frieda and the children. I wondered what would happen to them now. Two men finally caught my eye; they were dressed in civilian clothes, but I sensed they were soldiers because they did not look like the rest. Their faces, bearing, and haunted eyes gave them away.

Peter whispered to me, worriedly.

"Kurt? Will they really take us to Siberia?"

I turned to my young neighbor, finding myself stunned by the deep blue eyes, pale hair, and innocent expression. His eyes reminded me of my brother, Walter, who now lay dead somewhere in the Caucasus. The resemblance was remarkable and I had to force myself back to reality.

"I don't know, Peter, I sure hope not."

He stretched himself full length on the floor, and after a little while asked,

"Kurt?"

"Hm?"

"I'm scared."

I answered back in the same hushed tone, "Don't be ashamed of it. So am I."

"Really?"

"Really."

Peter fell silent and before long I heard his deep, even breathing. That night I promised myself that I would keep an eye on him.

The sun had already set, and as no light penetrated the room it soon became dark. Gradually the whispering died out in the room, but still sleep wouldn't come. I let my thoughts wander back to friends, and the past. Life was a mystery. I tried very hard to pray, but somehow could not manage it. There was a barrier within me. Later, when I wanted to turn on my side, I discovered my hands folded peacefully over my chest. I smiled happily at this, and soon fell asleep.

I was awakened the next morning by the sound of heavy boots tramping up the stairs. A soldier came in and loudly made us understand we were to go downstairs and wait in line.

"Dawai! Dawai!" (Get moving!) It was my first experience with this word, but for years it would be for me the most hated word in the Russian language.

As we hurried down, I whispered to Peter, "Stay with me. Don't leave my side."

He nodded his head and nearly crawled into my pockets.

The Russians began placing us in marching position, and counting heads. Each time they counted, they arrived at a different figure.

After a long while, they finally agreed on a number. Under heavy guard, we marched away from the compound. At the village square we turned right, coming out on a highway leading to the village of Bolzen, several kilometers away. There was just a touch of spring in the air.

Enroute, we encountered several different Russian vehicles. The trucks stormed by noisily almost driving us into the ditch while mocking soldiers shook their fists at us and shouted triumphantly, *"Hitler Kaput!"* The dust nearly choked us.

After abour an hour of marching, a halt was called. A Russian soldier spoke to us and to my surprise, Peter answered him. He spoke haughtily to Peter, who nodded several times to show that he understood. Finally, Peter told us,

"We will have a fifteen minute rest period. The guards stand ready to kill anyone who walks farther than twenty paces. That's about all!"

Peter sat down and I regarded him with curiosity. He explained that his parents spoke Russian and Polish.

"Well!" I exclaimed, "You'll be able to put it to good use where we're going!"

"On your feet, Germanskies! *Dawai!*"

We were on the move again, arriving in Bolzen sometime in the afternoon. I had the impression that an evacuation had occurred here, too, because very few civilians but plenty of Rusian soldiers were present. We were led to a large farm where many more prisoners were being held. In the central square, surrounded by barns and farm buildings, a huge fire was burning while prisoners sat around roasting potatoes in the embers.

Russian guards were all over the place; but they let us alone. We squeezed between the other prisoners, taking a few potatoes without being invited.

We were allowed to sleep anywhere we wanted to in the camp, and as far as food was concerned, that was our responsibility.

The day before, a prisoner had been caught too far away from the farm and the guards assumed he had tried to escape. They gave him a brutal beating as an example to the others.

We saw him upon entering the house. I could see from Peter's reaction that he was still inexperienced with the results of violence. He stared horrified at the man, and it was a long time before he adjusted to the sight. I pulled him away and together we investigated the house. We found there was plenty from to sleep in the attic. We looked systematically from top to bottom; there was not much left by this time — a glass of marmalade, some salt, and some fruits preserves.

In the cellar we found a pot of goose fat — if we only had some bread! As I stretched out in the attic to think for awhile, an idea began to develop in my mind.

"Peter", I asked, casually, "What's the Russian word for bread?"

"*Xleb*."

"Do you think we can make a deal with the Russians?"

He was gently sarcastic, "What do *you* have to offer?"

He was right; I had ideas, but nothing concrete to offer. I stood up, looking absently through the window. From a building on the left, two Russians were leading a cow down a path to their quarters. Suddenly, I had my inspiration! What is good enough for them, is good for us, I thought, calling Peter over to the window.

"Do you see those Russians with the cow?" I asked.

"Yes. What of it??'

'I'm sure they're going to slaughter the poor creature. That means the kitchen will be busy for a while. What we have to do," I continued, as he still did not understand, 'is to get into the kitchen!"

"But", he asked naively, "how are we going to accomplish that?"

'My dear friend, that is your job! You speak Russian, don't you?"

"So?"

"Go down and speak to that gentleman in uniform over there, ask him if he can arrange for you to see the commandant."

"What should I say then?"

"That we are hungry and want to work in the kitchen."

Now he liked my plan and became very excited; before I could stop him, he had almost run out the door.

"Hey!" I called out, "Don't forget you have a buddy here who loves to eat, too."

He grimaced, waved his hand, and was out the door in a flash. I saw him approach the sentry, and said to myself,

"Peter, my young friend, you're doing all right. But the fight for survival has just begun."

Some time passed without any sign of Peter and I began to doubt the value of my plan. Then I saw him coming back to the house, his face wreathed in smiles. He dashed up the stairs puffing excitedly. Greatly enjoying his role as a successful soldier, he snapped to attention, and saluted authoritatively, exclaiming,

"Mission accomplished! We are to report to the kitchen tomorrow morning on the double!"

His chest swelled with pride and he paraded around

the room like a peacock. At this moment, even the sight of his release papers would not have made him happier.

The Russian kitchen was outside the camp, but still on the farm grounds. We were situated on the kind of estate known as a *"Gut"*, common to this part of the country. It was a huge farm covering several square miles, many times the size of a farm like Frau Arnheim's, for example. The kitchen was about half a mile from where we were stationed.

A soldier escorted us to the kitchen. When the *Starschi* (Chief Cook) met us, he asked if we understood Russian. Peter spoke up, and our assignments were communicated through him. I assumed correctly that kitchen duties were the same in any army. Also, I was right, the cow had been slaughtered and there was lots of work to do.

We worked diligently, showing good intentions, and the *Starschi* pronounced himself satisfied with our work, giving us plenty to eat. He offered us some Russian *Machorka* (tobacco) which is coarse and green. It was totally new to me, and I rolled it in a piece of Russian newspaper with an experienced hand. However, I was not prepared, for its peculiar impact. I'm sure the first puff tore a hole in my lung the size of a fist. The *Starschi* was very amused, asking me repeatedly,

"Choroscho? Choroscho?" (Is good?)

I already knew what this word meant from Peter, and I was about to reply affirmatively, when I was stopped by a fit of coughing.

The good-humored *Starschi* doubled over with laughter, the tears running down his face.

But we returned home that day with half a loaf of bread each and full stomachs. And for a few days after that, food was no problem. In fact, we were even able to use the surplus for trading purposes. For half a loaf of bread and a bowl of soup, I obtained a rucksack which stayed with me all the way to Siberia. Peter came into possession of a handsome patchwork blanket which he treasured, and was heart-broken when the guards later took it from him.

The camp was filling up with prisoners, all in civilian clothes. When darkness fell, the activity was disturbing. The Russians, shouting and shooting their rifles into the air, chased everyone into the building. No one was allowed outside.

The next morning when we reported as usual for kitchen duty, there were three more prisoners to work with us. Also, this time, when I tried one of *Starschi's* "Machorcka-grenades", I only coughed half as much.

Later on several prisoners held a conference to discuss the possibility of escape. I led Peter away from them, advising him not to indulge in such day-dreams.

"For the time being, this is the safest place. The Russians are everywhere. It would be impossible to avoid them. There's no point in looking like that fellow on the couch."

That morning, he and another sick prisoner were transferred out of the camp to places unknown.

One morning, we were stopped on the way to the kitchen. A Russian guard pointed his gun at us, shouting, "*Nazat! Nazat!*" (Go back!) Peter grabbed me by the sleeve and told me we'd better return to the camp. It did not take long for us to learn the reason for this.

We could see the centre of the yard from the windows of the attic, there two officers had assembled several Russian and Polish soldiers. Peter and I ran down not to miss anything. A Polish officer spoke to us in German, saying camp was to be broken in fifteen minutes and we should line up in marching formation. Ironically, he added that we had shown exemplary discipline and he expected us to continue to show it! He stamped, swearing he would tolerate no foolishness.

Despite his excellent speech, I must say that the prisoners, were not in the kind of shape that should be displayed on a parade ground. The Russians used much cursing, slapping, and hitting with their rifle butts, to mold us into a presentable formation.

Then the counting began, and as the number came out wrong each time, we stood there for an eternity. Somehow, by abstruse methods, the soldiers settled on a compromise figure, and after much shouting and display of authority, they ordered, *"Dawai Marsch!"*

The column moved out into the street while a Polish officer rode past, his open carriage driven by his second in command. It could have been a chariot out of Ben Hur, as he applied his whip indiscriminately to our backs.

As we left the compound, I noticed the *Starschi,* puffing his *Machorka* and moving his head about as though looking for someone; I wondered if it could have been Peter.

The Polish officer set a bone-breaking pace for us. It might have been different if the column had consisted only of experienced soldiers; but it was mostly composed of elderly male civilians, who could not keep up the murderous pace. Many carried useless ballast on their backs, demonstrating their ignorance of forced marching. Disaster was in the air from the moment we left the *Gut*.

After a short time, the formation lost all semblance of order, leaving large gaps in the lines. The Polish officer cursed and swung his whip against the prisoners, driving them like sheep to close the ranks. People who had fallen behind received similar treatment from the rear guards. A halt was called about 15 kilometers away from the camp. Many were already limping; I noticed the strain on their faces. The Polish officer looked at the long, dishevelled column, then he called his soldiers together for instructions. I had a fairly good idea of what the instructions were.

We rested for a longer time than I expected. It seemed strange that we should be pushed so hard for 15 kilometers, only to be given such a long rest period. This was soon explained by a cloud of dust coming from the direction of a nearby village. A column of about forty new prisoners was being driven forward at an unbelievable pace.

I was astonished at Peter who did not show any strain. I turned to him anxiously, saying,

"Before the day is over, there'll be some excitement. The signs are everywhere."

Without raising his head, he replied "I'm not bored."

Peter's dry remark surprised me, and I suggested we work our way to the head of the column, where the pace was set. This would eliminate the running, and perhaps the whip, too.

The new prisoners were given hardly any rest at all. We had to assemble on the road again. The Polish Napoleon stood in his carriage, giving the order to march and cracking his whip, while the line of suffering flesh moved on.

We marched through a desolate country ravaged by war. There was ruin and devastation everywhere we looked.

Der Hergott gab uns ein Paradies, doch wir menschen verwandelten es zveiner Hölle!

The Lord gave man a Paradise, but he turned it into a bloody Hell!

During the entire infamous march, we were given nothing to drink. Stagnant water lay in ditches along the side of the road. Beside them, or even in them, lay the bloated remains of livestock. We had to resist the temptation to drink this polluted water, because of the deadly danger.

We passed a village in which the women had placed pails of drinking water along the roadside for us, but the Polish guards took savage delight in kicking them over, so their precious contents spilled out into the sand. I told Peter to chew on a jacket button; this would produce enough saliva to keep him going.

Men fell to the roadside and were brutally forced to their feet. As we walked, the road filled with the excess baggage cast off by the marchers. Next to us was a man in his early fifties who struggled manfully with a heavy sack over his shoulder. I asked him why he didn't get rid of it. He explained that inside it were eight loaves of bread. I offered to carry the load for him in exchange for two loaves — he agreed. I gave Peter my rucksack and threw the bundle over my shoulder. Almost immediately, the man grew two inches taller.

One elderly man had reached his limit and fell to the ground, opened his shirt, and pleaded with the Polish officer,

"Shoot me! I can't go on! I want to die!"

I do not know what happened to him, but I heard no shots. At last we were granted a rest. I estimated we had marched twenty five kilometers. They had taken their toll. Men lay around in pitiful condition, and the one who had given me his package collapsed in his tracks from complete exhaustion. His face was flushed and the veins throbbed in his temples.

Peter was still in good shape. I was relieved not to have to worry about him. I was surprised that I did not feel the strain as much as I had expected, either. We still had a few glasses of preserves and juice with us and opened them greedily. When Peter and I had finished, he nodded his head toward the old man. I assented, giving him the remainder of the preserves. He thanked us, saying, "You are two good comrades." Then he gave us our two loaves of bread which Peter put into our rucksack.

While we sat there, the remainder of the stragglers caught up with the group. The guards, angrily pushed them along with curses and beatings. This, of course, accomplished nothing — these men were exhausted. The Polish officer paced back and forth along the column, kicking the prisoners, and shaking his pistol in their faces. He did not use it, however, but he raved like an animal. Then he spit a few times, climbed on top of his wagon, riding off, furiously swinging his whip in every direction. The rest period was over.

Men halted along the road and it was a long time before we were in marching formation again. The Polish Napoleon now had a splendid idea and gesticulated with his arms like a conductor, shouting,

"Singen! 'Es ist so schön Soldat zu sein! Eins, Zwei, Drei!"

Of course, the result was lamentable. Most of us could hardly breathe, let alone sing! The officer worked himself up into a red fury. A shot sounded in the rear of the column and many heads turned to find out what happened, but nothing could be seen from my position.

We arrived at a village late in the afternoon of this unforgettable day. We were taken to a farm where there was good well water. After we had drunk our fill, we were driven into a big barn. Warnings were issued saying that anyone who tried to escape would be shot. We were given nothing to eat, but fortunately Peter and I had our two loaves. That night I slept like a dead man.

The next morning the first sounds we heard were screams and shouts, as orders were given to assemble in the farm quadrangle.

During the night one of the older prisoners had hanged himself from a rafter. The Polish Napoleon swore the man was a coward and consequently we would all have to pay the price of his death because we had not stopped him. At this moment while I begged for God's blessing, I could only hear the Devil's laughter.

The punishment came directly.

From the way we were being driven at a brisk pace I knew that the march would collapse in an hour and a half at the most.

It surprised me that the Polish officer had enough compassion to take about a half dozen men, unable to march, into a wagon which he had confiscated from another farm. Perhaps he thought they'd slow us down, but undoubtedly he had his orders from higher up, and personally went through the column selecting only those who were clearly at the gates of death.

As I predicted, the formation broke down completely after the first six kilometers. The officer swung his whip, but this did not improve the situation. Reluctantly, he picked a few more up with the wagon. Several men begged to be shot; the sight was dreadful; a picture of total misery.

The same scenes were repeated all day as we marched from village to village. When we reached the City of Landsberg, we were given warm soup and two days rest.

We were broken up into groups, searched, and interrogated. Peter and I stayed as close together as Siamese twins.

During the interrogation, I told the same story as I had told in the beginning. By now, I knew it so well I could repeat it in my sleep.

When we were called up again to join a marching formation, we were put into a small column of seventy men. Our destination? Unknown. But we were marching towards Frankfurt. To our great relief, the Polish Napoleon had left us — Hallelujah and good riddance!

It was mid-afternoon when we marched into Frankfurt on the Oder. The streets were almost deserted; and we marched up to a large house. Once inside, we were taken through a long, brightly lit corridor, down some stairs, into a basement. There was barely enough room for all seventy of us; but they locked us in the cellar, leaving us scared and apprehensive.

We had only enough room to lie down on our sides with our legs drawn under us. After the door was locked, the cellar became pitch black because there was no light from the street, since the windows were boarded up. Peter and I stumbled around, and found ourselves a corner at the back of the cellar, away from the door. Exhausted from the march, we fell asleep instantly.

Suddenly from the depths of sleep, I sat bolt upright. A horrible scream had pierced the night, and with it the sound of angry Russian voices. Repeatedly, I heard dull blows, more screams, and more voices. I felt Peter tremble beside me.

By this time, everyone was awake, and the sound of murmuring filled the cellar. Fear and grim foreboding kept us wide awake for hours.

Someone removed the boards from the window, and let in the morning light. Then the door sprang open, and in the frame of the doorway, was an ogre more terrible than the Devil's son.

He stood with his feet masterfully planted against the side of the doorway, and rocked back and forth on the soles of his boots. A leer of malicious hatred and implacable scorn was on his lips, and ugly scars ran from his cheeks to his temples, while black eyes pierced our souls. His hands were set squarely on his hips, and from his left one, dangled a black riding whip.

We sat numbly, waiting for his next move. It came suddenly; the whip blazed from his hand, striking us, swift as lightning. Cries of anguish rose from the prisoners. Wherever it fell, the whip hit its target with a crack of thunder.

After this vengeful god had sated his sadistic appetite, he shouted in good German,

"Listen, swine! my name is Ivan! The next time I enter this room, everyone to his feet! The first man that sees me yells, *Achtung!* Everybody up! Hands at their sides and hats off!"

He slapped whip against his riding boots, while his stocky frame shook from side to side. He was our hangman, and when he leered, the cruel scars bulged out, grotesquely.

"German pigs! All knives, forks and other sharp objects on the floor!" He cracked the whip, saying, "I will return in five minutes!" The door slammed behind him.

By this time, few of us had any sharp instrument left. The Russian guards had scoured away everything but the lice on our shirts. We waited quietly for a half hour before Ivan returned again. The desperate anxiety created by the long delay was unbearable.

When Ivan the Terrible (as we called him from this moment on) returned, he sneered at the "deadly weapons" we had amassed beside the door.

"Is that all?" he shouted, ready to whip us because the heap was so small. He frowned, and the muscles in his ugly face worked uneasily. Then he ordered us out of the cellar into the courtyard we were helped along by punches and kicks administered by Russian and Polish soldiers.

CHAPTER FOUR

The courtyard was a large gravel square surrounded by high stone walls, where a large number of Russian and Polish soldiers stood about. They frisked us again, and everything seemed to be in order, until a nail file was discovered on one of the prisoners.

Before our horrified eyes, he was pummelled, kicked, and spat upon to excess. After the soldiers had finished with him, they lined up in two opposite rows, waiting for us. It seemed that the fun was just beginning.

Running the Gauntlet! Just like in the days of Frederick the Great!

They swung at us with their closed fists and other objects, working themselves into a frenzy, as we ran in pain and humiliation back to the cellar. I was able to dodge many blows, managing to get back without being seriously injured, but Peter had a big welt on his forehead. He swore like a trooper.

As we returned to our cellar, we discovered that everything had been searched. A short while later, the door opened, and a large bowl of soup with half dozen loaves of bread were set down before us. Then the door was slammed shut.

We reacted to the food like caged animals. Our struggles to reach the food, resulted in chaos. Everyone was shouting and pushing towards the front of the cellar. The bread was torn into bits immediately. A man cried out in pain; he had been pushed by the surging crowd, and stood with one foot in the boiling soup, causing it to spill onto the floor, losing much of it.

Only those with some sort of container had any hope of getting some soup. Peter and I considered ourselves lucky to grab a piece of bread no larger than a man's fist.

In the midst of this confusion, a leader emerged. A man, unnoticed before, stood up and shouted,

"Ruhe !" ("Silence !")

His voice had a deep ring to it. He repeated his command twice, before we quieted down. Then he spoke to us indignantly,

"Men! Have you all gone mad? Your actions are disgraceful, unworthy of men!"

The was some muttering, but he shouted again,

"Silence!"

He pointed a finger towards the door.

"This is exactly what the Russians want! Disunity! Let's not make it easy for them!"

Some men murmured, while others nodded silently. We all knew he was right. He continued,

"Listen, all of you. The next time the food arrives, everyone remains where he is. I'll distribute the food, and see to it that everyone receives his share." He looked defiantly at the door, "We'll show them a thing or two!"

He sat down again in the straw and chewed on a piece of bread. I had a good chance to look him over, now. His eyes revealed tremendous will power. His heavy beard lent dignity to his appearance. Despite his being in civilian clothes, he was every inch a military leader. If my memory was accurate, I had seen this man before, and in German uniform, too!

Ivan the Terrible stood in the doorway, and someone yelled "*Achtung!*"

We stood rooted to the spot while an ugly glow of satisfaction covered his face.

"German pigs learn manners quickly!" He held a list in his hand, and called out a name. Someone answered, "Here!"

"Come to me!" Ivan snapped.

When this man approached, he grabbed him by the scruff of the neck, "From now on, when I call someone's name, he will answer, "Here, *Mein Fuehrer!*" because I am your Fuehrer now! Is that clear?"

Our silence showed that we understood.

"*Dawai!*" The door slammed.

Waiting for Ivan to return was nerve wracking, and he did return four times more to pick up prisoners. None of them came back to our dungeon. This went on all day and into the night.

Late in the afternoon, as we could judge from the sun streaming through the window bars, Ivan the Terrible popped in again; this time he called,

"Dombrowski, Peter!"

Peter was rigid with fear. There was a second of deadly silence when I felt him tremble. Quickly I whispered, "Here, *Mein Fuehrer!*"

Peter repeated it in a choked voice.

"Come along boy, quickly!" Ivan shouted, indiscriminately swinging his whip about. The door slammed shut after them.

My heart was full of worry for Peter and I tried to believe they would not hurt him. He was too young to have been involved in anything; but like the others, he did not come back.

There was no doubt left in my mind, that we were in the claws of the feared N.K.V.D. (also known as the G.P.U.), the mighty Soviet Secret Police. There is a saying in Russia that two things always succeed — the N.K.V.D. and the Russian Railroad.

Ivan returned and invited us, sardonically, to the latrine. Once out in the yard, we discovered his motives — running the gauntlet again! We crowded together like frightened sheep; but the crack of his whip soon made us move. The blows fell on us like hail. In their great eagerness to hit us, the soldiers hindered one another. This saved us from some painful blows. I was able to dodge most of the blows, but was not fast enough to dodge a powerful kick in the rear. I was booted so powerfully, the trip of the latrine was no longer necessary.

Thus passed our first day of initiation into the methods of the N.K.V.D. — starvation, brutality, and lack of sleep. We received no more food that day. Towards night, Ivan installed a powerful light bulb in the ceiling. It burned all night to keep us awake.

The interrogations continued through the night, and Ivan's zeal to punish us increased as the night wore on. He was marvellously inventive in devising new ways to have "fun" with us. His whip fell on our backs for the smallest infractions, and sometimes for no reason at all.

I once believed I couldn't hate any man as much as my platoon sergeant; but Ivan the Terible taught me the true meaning of hatred. I felt a shudder penetrate my soul at the very sight of him. Nothing else has ever produced this feeling in me.

As our numbers were slowly diminishing, space became available in the cellar; I could now stretch out in the straw. Lying on my back, I struggled with my anxiety about the coming interrogation. What would happen to me, if they discovered my story was a pack of lies?

Ivan returned with his roster of names, and after slapping us around a bit, he called out,

"Stock, Kurt!"

My wildly beating heart nearly jumped out of my throat, but I pulled myself together and yelled,

"Here, *Mein Fuehrer!*"

I was dealt a solid blow accompanied by a curse. Outside I was met by a Russian soldier and led down a corridor and up a stairway. My guide stopped before a heavy wooden door and knocked. After a Russian voice answered, he opened it, motioning me inside.

The room was lit by one screened bulb in the ceiling. The walls were a bleak yellow and the room almost empty. Directly opposite me was a large desk; on which sat an enormously tall Russian officer, smoking a cigarette. Beside him stood a Polish officer, while against the left wall leaned a bundle of walking canes.

It appeared as if the two officers had forgotten me, they were so preoccupied with a piece of paper. After an unbearable wait, the Pole turned and looked me over slowly. Coming over, he pointed to a stool next to the door, against the wall. After I sat down, he offered me a cigarette. I had only dragged on it a few times, when the Russian said,

"*Kak familja!*"

As I stared at him blankly, the Pole asked in perfect German,

"What is your name?"

He took over the interrogation.

"Born when and where?"

"Thirtieth of November, 1920, Berlin."

"Were you ever a member of the N.S.D.A.P.?"

"No."

His open hand hit me in the face like a bolt of lightning, almost knocking me off my stool. The cigarette flew out of my hand while a powerful light directed from the desk blazed into my face. From somewhere the Pole shouted,

"Lies have short legs! We know all about you! I suggest that from now on you tell us the truth!"

The next question came like a pistol shot:

"What was your position in the Hitler Youth?"

"I was never a member." I answered truthfully.

My answers seemed to displease him and my head crashed against the wall. This time he hit me with his clenched fist right between the eyes. The room began to spin, and I fell into a bottomless pit.

Terrible pains in my ribs brought me back to consciousness. I lay on the floor, while the Russian and Polish officers used me like a football. Next, I was pulled by the hair and thrown back on the stool; my face again pushed into the spotlight.

Now I saw the Russian officer coming closer to me. He leaned so close, I smelt his bad breath. His lips were drawn back, revealing four capped silver teeth in his upper jaw. I almost blacked out again. Through his clenched teeth, he hissed,

"S.S.?"

"No, I was not an S.S. man." I croaked hoarsely.

In a vicious rage, he rushed to the left wall and grabbed a cane. The Pole dragged me from the stool, threw me to my knees, and rammed my head between his legs, holding me as in a vise.

The Russian removed my jacket and shirt, grabbing my arms as he looked desperately for the "SS" tattoo. Disappointed, he swung the cane, beating my back like a madman. The pain was terrifying! My back burned like fire.

At the beginning, I cried out but as the beating became more vicious, I only groaned like a wounded animal. That night something was smashed inside of me, which to this day has not been completely healed.

My pride, honor, and self-confidence as a man.

I had built a house of lies, but ironically, I had told them nothing but the truth! From nowhere the Pole spoke.

"You will have plenty of time to think it over and tell us the truth next time!"

With a solid kick, I was dismissed. The aide was called, and I was dragged out the door. He pushed me to my feet, stuffed my shirt into my jacket pocket, throwing it over my shoulders. I stumbled down the hall like a drunkard. The guard yelled,

"Dawai! Dawai! Bistra!"

When we came to the staircase, I grabbed the railing so that I would not fall down the stairs. The soldier let me catch my breath as he lit a cigarette. Looking cautiously about, he whispered,

"Dawai, Fritz, Kurietje!" (Hurry, Fritz, smoke!)

He held the cigarette to my lips. The Russians often called us "Fritz", just as we called them "Ivan".

After a few drags, he took the cigarette away, stamping it out. Loudly, he shouted, *"Dawai! Dawai!"*, and helped me down the stairs. Once in the cellar, he led me down the corridor. We passed two prison cells, stopping at the third.

Ivan came running out, grinning like the Devil, an enormous key-ring in his hand. The steel door creaked open, and I was admitted to my new accomodations. Ivan gave me a tremendous shove on my back making me cry out in agony. The door was slammed and locked again, and I sank into the straw, on my stomach.

Peter's anxious voice was close to my ear,

"Kurt! What have they done to you?"

I rose slowly, resting on my hands and knees. Peter looked at me, stupefied! I tried to smile, but couldn't. He must have thought me insane, which was not far from the truth. Physically and spiritually, I was damaged almost beyond repair. For a glass of water, I would have sold my soul to the devil! The fear dried up every cell in my body.

Peter was a true comrade; he would have borne half my pain if he could. He was the only person able to rouse my feeble will to live. My back burned with pain the skin as cut and covered with blood.

My joints seemed to be functioning and no bones were broken. Peter later told me about his interrogation. They were interested mainly in his Polish name and his ancestory. He answered the questions in Polish as best he could. Apparently the officers were satisfied. When asked about his activities in the past few months, he ingenuously told them that he had been digging trenches for the army. With that they let him go.

The door opened and a man sailed in. He was the one who had made himself our leader in the other cellar. His nose bled heavily, and hardly was the door closed, when he began swearing a blue streak,

"Filthy pimps-assholes-pisspots!"

With a dirty handkerchief he tried to staunch the bleeding.

My memory was not damaged after all; I knew him immediately. In the Spring of 1943, I attended a non-commissioned officer's course 25 miles from the front at Alakurty. Sergeant Kindermann was famous for his colorful expressions, which seemed to be infinite in number.

"In my day," he would say, "We had sergeant material! We were really men; for breakfast we ate nails, and spikes for dinner. And at night we fucked heavy women! Yes, sir, those were times! It was an honor to wear the German uniform then. You meatheads, today, don't know a thing. But be assured, you'll hate the day you were born when I'm through with you!"

He proved that he meant every word of it. Kindermann was the toughest, meanest sergeant anyone could have, but he was a great soldier.

Spiess Kindermann came over to our corner and sat down in the straw, leaning his back against the wall. I crawled about, looking for a more comfortable position. As I groaned with pain, Kindermann looked at me, saying,

"They didn't handle you with kid gloves either, did they?"

"No. We wouldn't agree on a few points. Those two slimy Russians became damn unfriendly, especially the one with the silver mine in his face; he knew all the answers! You know, he's a hostile son-of-a-bitch!"

The sergeant's face was drawn up in a swollen mass of flesh.

"Man," he moaned, "your humor is too much!"

"I know. Looking at you gives me all the inspiration I need."

This banter enabled us to establish communication. We spoke a pure infantry dialect, common to our regiment. No matter how great the danger, or bad the situation, we gave ourselves strength with our irreverent language.

No man ever learned how to die. That is one thing the army cannot drill into you. Yet, we stood with one foot in the pine box every day, waiting for our one way ticket to Hell. I remember how many soldiers I had known who died in combat. Some of them disciplined themselves for a last salute before dying, while others said something brave or honorable, an expression of inner peace on their lips. They had not only mastered the art of living, but the art of dying as well!

After the war, people talked a great deal about the so-called premonitions of soldiers. I'd like to relate my own personal experience.

It was in Finland, and our batallion was preparing to launch an assault to recapture a mountain position of great strategic importance. It had changed hands several times, never without great rivers of blood being shed for it. Although we knew this could mean our "one-way trip", we joked like fools, trying to maintain the pretense that nothing serious was involved.

Someone said,

"Listen, you guys, I've got it all figured out. We're going up that hill as if it were merely a Sunday afternoon stroll."

"It's alright by me," a soldier retorted, "The mountain air is just what my doctor prescribed."

A short, shifty-eyed character from Berlin regarded him with mock astonishment,

"Has your doctor lost his marbles? The air up there has too much lead in it!"

Werner Schramm, Private First Class, sat silently by himself. In the white afternoon, the shadows which played across his face made it seem composed of trenches and fox-holes of some no-man's land. I knelt beside my long-time buddy, asking,

"What do you think of this deal we've got again?"

Without giving me as much as a glance, he said tonelessly,

"It's a raw deal all right, expecially for me."

"Why do you say that Werner?"

"I can't explain why I feel my time is up."

I tried to make him forget this nonsense, but he ignored my optimistic words. Regarding me with empty eyes, he interjected,

"It's no use, Kurt, as I said I cannot explain it!"

A look of piety spread over his war-tired face as he spoke of his wife and children. Then tenderness faded as quickly as the sun hiding behind a cloud. The ghastly message of death was written in every line of his face, and the last words I heard him say were, "So long, Kurt. Take care of yourself."

Later, I passed him on the hill. He was lying face upwards; a large fragment of mortar had torn his throat, probably killing him instantly. His words returned, chilling me.

Kindermann recognized me for what I was, and whispering softly, he asked what batallion I belonged to. I told him.

"First class outfit." he replied, reluctantly.

"Smashed outfit would be more accurate." I corrected him.

Kindermann still was unaware we had met before, so I reminded him of the Unteroffizier's Course in 1943. He looked at me thoughtfully, then asked,

"Weren't you the bird brain that had the argument with one of my instructors ?"

I smiled with embarrassment, "It was me alright!"

"That cost you your stripes, nincompoop!"

At that time I decided he was being unfair so, jokingly, I offered to punch him in the nose. He didn't think it was funny and promptly reported me. I was chastised by both Kindermann and the Commanding officer. To top it off, I had to apologize to him. This seemed to satisfy him, and he withdrew his report. But I remained a private, first class.

The steel door was opened, and another helpless bundle flew across the floor. It continued like this for the rest of the night. I could not sleep, convinced that I would be next. My back hurt me terribly, so that no position was endurable for long.

Somehow the night passed, by now almost everyone had been transferred to the new dungeon. Next morning, the door opened, and a Russian sergeant entered. He did not speak German, but pointing towards the cellar door, he screamed, *"Dawai!"* With his right hand he made a motion to urinate. We were going to our morning exercise — the gauntlet. The mere thought of it made my teeth chatter.

The Russian bullies shouted their greetings as we entered the yard. They were eager to practise their pugilistic skills on us once more, and the first blow sent me sprawling to the ground. Peter ran quickly behind me and helped me to my feet. Then he stayed close to me, shielding my back with his, taking many blows on himself that were intended for me. When finally we reached the latrines, I discovered that I had fouled myself during the ordeal.

When we returned to the cellar at last, I tried to express my gratitude to Peter for his heroic assistance. He grinned self-deprecatingly, "It's nothing. Nothing at all."

Kindermann had suffered painfully, however. He

knelt in the straw, panting heavily. When he mustered up enough strength, he said,

"You're right, Kurt. That boy is okay."

"I recommend him for corporal immediately." I added.

Kindermann smiled, despite his pain.

The daily cabbage soup and the loaves of bread were sent down. Kindermann pulled himself to his feet; there was no weakness in his voice; that magnificent roar echoed through the room, as he ordered many impatient hands away from the food. His bushy black beard and swollen nose gave him the appearance of a patriarch standing before the soup as though defending his own life — a true sergeant-major of the old school!

No one dared make a move before we counted off. Finally, soup was distributed, and the bread torn into small pieces with the help of a spoon.

We had scarcely finished our miserable breakfast, when the Russian sergeant returned. The interrogations were beginning again. With the exception of nine men, whose fate we never learned, everyone interrogated was returned to our cell.

One prisoner returned from the interrogations, wandering about the cell like a deranged man. His eyes were dull and stared into space. In his left hand, he held a pair of smashed glasses, while his right arm dangled loosely by his side, as if no longer attached to his body.

At first, he was unaware of his surroundings. We spoke to him, but received no answer. At last, he began slowly to relate his story.

During the nineteen thirties, when the middle class in Germany experienced prosperity, it was considered the "freely-chosen duty" for the small business man to join the party. It was a case of joining the wolf-pack or being devoured by it. Then he followed the stream, prospered, and rose in the party ranks. It was "good business" then, but today his party membership brought him nothing but evil. Under the interrogation, he broke down and confessed; they made him sign a confession, then ordered him to raise his right arm in a German salute. As he held this position, a cane systematically smashed his arm.

When it was time for me to return to the lion's den, I walked through the grey prison corridors shuddering, a ring of ice around my heart.

I was admitted to the same room and sat down on the same stool as before. This time there was no cigarette.

"For your sake, we hope you have decided to tell us the truth today!" the Pole sneered.

"I have." I mustered a note of confidence into my voice.

"Really? We shall see."

The spotlight was turned on full force, blinding me.

"Were you a soldier?"

"Yes."

"Rank and unit?"

"Obergefreiter 1st Battalion, 307th Regiment, 163rd Division."

"Where did you last see action?"

"Finland."

Silvertooth rose from his chair and came around the desk. He leaned over me, lit a cigarette, and playfully blew smoke into my face.

"What was the duration of your service?" The Pole continued.

Considering my civilian clothes, I felt the best course open to me was to fall back on my old story.

"I served from 1940 to 1943."

"What did you do from 1943 until you were captured?"

"My brother was killed in Russia; this made me the only surviving son in our family. According to Hitler's order, only one son in a family was withdrawn from front line duty and given reclamation work. I was discharged from the army and put to work in a munitions plant."

"In Berlin?"

"Yes."

"Why is it then, in March this year, you were captured in Pomerania?"

My temples pounded, and my mouth was as dry as dust. I was afraid my behavior would expose me. Only with the greatest willpower did I conceal my agitation and continue with my story.

"We lost our home in an air raid, and were evacuated to Pomerania."

The Pole did not buy my story. He discussed the situation with Silvertooth who wanted to get at me in his own way. The Pole shot questions at me with great rapidity, without giving me time to make up answers.

"Were you a member of the N.S.D.A.P.?"

"No."

"Volksstorm?"

"No!"

"Werwolf?"

"No!"

He ran down a list of organizations I had no idea existed. Silvertooth was ready to burst with impatience as he panted like a walrus. Finally, he spun around and ran to the corner where his beloved canes were stacked. Waving the sturdiest one under my nose, he hissed,

"S.S.?"

"No!" I cried out, panic-stricken.

Suddenly, a piercing pain split my head open and my lower jaw felt as if it had been torn away from skull. My lips swelled up and there was a jarring pain in my gums. Blood collected in my mouth which I almost spit into his bestial face.

Apparently Silvertooth had read my mind because he grabbed my hair, and in a sadistic rage slammed my head repeatedly against the wall. Mercifully I felt myself being swallowed up into the painless darkness.

I must have been unconscious for a long time because the voices of the two officers seemed very far away. My head was a tortured mass of pain and blood.

"Dawai! Dawai!" A soldier shouted into my ear as he dragged me out of the room, away from my torturers.

How I made it back to the cell, I'll never know. When I fell on to the straw, my head was filled with the buzzing of a million bees.

Now, I reached the point where the will to live disappeared. I was no longer a human being, I was merely a suffering mass of flesh, with no sense of the past or future. In my tortured mind, I saw no relief except in death. I could not endure another session of brutality. And what about my past? It had been bruised, spat upon, and ripped to shreds by every means available to man. There wasn't a man left now, just a shell, a bundle of left overs.

For several days there was a lull. With the help of my two friends, Peter and Kindermann, I recovered slowly. My cheekbones were cracked and bruised, my eyes half-closed, my mouth so sore that it was painful to even try to smile at their jokes. I didn't have to look in a mirror to see how I looked — I only had to look at the faces around me. They were battered just like mine.

I was given different jobs to do, in the beginning. One of them was to sweep the staircases in the barracks of the Polish officers. This was a bonanza in cigarette butts. Or it would have been if the guard hadn't hit me so frequently with his German sword when I bent over to pick up the butts. It also amused him to kick me in the rear. I wanted the butts desperately and I played this degrading game as I cleaned up the garbage and dirt. But the spirit suffers; it is never the same again. Then I was lucky. I was put on kitchen duty along with my two friends and we got out into the open air while we peeled potatoes. This helped my recovery.

It was our good fortune that the single guard was the same one who had given me the cigarette to smoke. He allowed us to converse with each other as long as our work did not slow down. Every once in a while he roared, *"Dawai!"* so that it echoed throughout the entire yard. Then he took out a pack of cigarettes, lit one, and put the rest back in such a way that it missed his pocket and fell to the ground. He appeared to look elsewhere, while we picked up the smokes.

To our inexpressible relief, the ordeal of running the gauntlet was stopped; this was certainly a sign from heaven. It gave us time to repair our shattered confidence, without having it torn to shreds again by this inhumane torture. During the next few days, I recovered from my depression. The time spent in the fresh air, freedom from nightly interrogations, and the irreplaceable friendship of Peter and Kindermann, all contributed to the restoration of my health in a short time.

Easter Sunday. The weather was beautiful, and the sun shone brightly. Our awakened desire for freedom was a powerful ache in our hearts. We sat in the yard peeling potatoes, looking up into the trees, watching the birds bustle about in the fresh green foliage. What a merry crew, I thought. There were no fetters on their wings. They acted like children, flying in and out among the trees and bushes, singing their untramelled song to the four corners of the earth.

Back in the cellar, we still had to contend with Ivan the Terrible. I believe that he was insane, and when he drank vodka, he was more dangerous than usual. He was always a step ahead of us, never visiting without some ingenious trick to play. But even he seemed to have slackened off, making us really grateful.

Our "convalescent leave" came to a sudden end when the interrogations resumed on the Tuesday after Easter. It was only a matter of bearing up under the tension while waiting to be called, and walking through the dismal corridors up to the interrogation room.

Each time I saw my questioners, they were more direct than before. Today, their welcoming gesture was a box on the ear. Meanwhile, I had learned their names; Silvertooth was called Larenkov; the Pole's name was Lewinsky.

Tovarich Lewinsky pounced on me right away, "You have lied to me again!"

I was not expected to answer that.

"We have collected more information on you in the past few days."

He lit a cigarette slowly, scrutinizing me with hate-filled eyes.

"Your statement that you were a civilian from 1943 to 1945 is a big lie!" Lewinsky pointed his finger at me, and screamed, "You were a soldier until the last day!"

I felt as if an alarm clock went off inside of me. My veins throbbed in every direction, while I struggled to think coherently. What did they want of me? A confession that I was a soldier until the last moment? That they could have, gladly. However, I guessed they wanted something more. Lewinsky drew himself up to his full height before me.

"The 163rd Division consists of three regiments, which one was yours?"

"The 307th."

"Isn't it strange, that the 307th Regiment was destroyed in the same area where you were captured? A funny coincidence, no?"

I remained silent. Lewinsky's pleasure at this cat and mouse game was written all over his face, and his voice broke with self-satisfaction when he asked:

"And what was your rank before you had the clever idea of changing into civilian clothes?"

"Obergefreiter." I answered truthfully. He gave me a powerful slap, that nearly threw me off the stool.

"You despicable liar! You cowardly mongrel! You were an officer! THAT'S why you disguised yourself in civilian clothes."

Lewinsky seemed on the brink of lunacy, and Tovarich Larenkov took over. Panting heavily, he whipped out his pistol and held the nozzle against my left temple as he shoved his Junkhans wristwatch under my nose.

"Minute!"

I had reached the limit of my endurance, and saw that it did not matter what I answered — either way, I was guilty. Tovarich Larenkov's trigger finger was itchy; my chances for a fair game of Russian roulette were nil.

Now only twenty seconds remained, and my brain was numb. I was bathed in sweat and the blood in my veins churned while my life ticked away with each second. God help me!

The minute was up, and I was in the hands of Fate. From a great distance came the poisonous hiss of Larnekov's voice,

"Offizier!"

"Nooo . . .!" I cried, shaking my head.

The dreaded shot did not come, and Larenkov cursed until his voice broke. Lifting his pistol, he struck the barrel against my head with a powerful back hand, and the room spun before my eyes, as blood ran down my left temple. I fell into a pit of blackness.

Peter was leaning over me; trying to push his leather jacket under my head as a pillow; Kindermann sat on the other side, holding a pot of water to my lips. Instinctively, I grabbed my head with both hands and rocked back and forth. There was a horrible swelling on my left temple. Peter said,

"When they brought you back, I thought you were dead."

"Nonsense", Kindermann waved him aside impatiently, "Don't worry about him. Only the good ones die."

Peter was aghast, but Kindermann was giving me the right medicine. He tore a piece of his shirt and used it to wash my wounds; then he emitted a slow whistle. When I looked at him quizzically, he said:

"I've reached the conclusion that those two piss-pots up there don't care for you too much."

"You're so right, we always get into some sort of scrap!"

"You were damn lucky this time, boy; but I suggest that in the future you look after your head better."

"Don't worry Spiess! The next time I'll wear my helmet."

Peter looked from Kindermann to me, amazed. Then he shook his head, as if to say,

"You're both nuts!"

Later another prisoner was brought back from interrogation. When he had recovered enough to talk, he told us his unbelievable story.

Larenkov had not treated him too badly in the previous interrogations, but it was his misfortune to have kept a picture of his family on himself. Larenkov studied it with great interest. In the picture were the prisoner, his brother, and his parents, all in civilian clothes. Suddenly Larenkov had an inspiration; he pointed to the brother, shouting triumphantly,

"S.S. Offizier?"

This conjecture gave everyone else in the picture a promotion and a place in the party. The terrified prisoner denied the accusations, but it was useless. Larenkov was adamant and supported his belief with the cane. Then came the trick with the pistol. At this, the prisoner fell apart, admitted everything, and was forced to sign a confession. But, he told us,

"My brother was not an "SS" man. He served in the Navy and was lost at sea in 1943!"

Ivan the Terrible returned. Glaring darkly, he called out a name from his list. It was Kindermann's turn. The Spiess shouted, "Here, *Mein Fuehrer!,*" and walked through the door.

I awaited his return with anxiety and dire expectation. After an eternity, the door opened and Kindermann flew in. Peter and I dashed to his aid. He was in deplorable shape; his empty eyes stared straight ahead, and his lips were tightly clenched. One glance told us all about what Larenkov's cane had accomplished this time. The blood drained out of Peter's face; and tears came to his eyes when he saw Kindermann's blood-stained shirt and wounded back.

There was not much we could do for Kindermann; a drink of stale water, a few puffs from a bitter cigarette butt, and make room for him to lick his wounds like an animal. It was up to him to draw on his emotional and physical reserves to sustain his life. I remembered how I crawled through the lowest feelings on my way to recovery.

The next morning came, and with it, bread and cabbage soup. I looked after the distribution of the rations. Kindermann was in bad shape; he could not stand up, and complained of sharp pains in his ribs. When Ivan came with the work call, we reported Kindermann sick. Ivan took one look and said,

"Choroscho. Nix arbeiten!"

These were the kindest words I ever heard from Ivan the Terrible.

Peter and I went to the kitchen as usual. Peter did a good job of keeping the cook amicable by speaking Russian to him. The cook even let us smuggle some food out of the kitchen for Kindermann.

Peter surprised me that night by producing a box of matches from his pocket. With a sly laugh, he handed them to me. During the day, I had swept the ground for cigarette butts which I rolled up into cigarettes and shared them with Kindermann.

The Spiess smoked with pleasure — a good sign. It was time to try some of our good "medicine" on him.

"What do you think, Spiess, shall we call up our lawyer and complain about the rough treatment here?"

Kindermann blew the smoke through his nose, and retorted weakly,

"Better no, Kurt. Those two jackasses up there are likely to cancel our weekend pass."

I breathed easily again; the Spiess was on the road to recovery.

Two days passed without any new developments, although we were still subjected to the daily exercises of Ivan the Terrible. His pranks were more of a nuisance than anything else by now. We played his game with clenched teeth while repeating, "Yes, Mein Fuehrer", and thus we eluded his accursed whip.

One night we returned from our evening trip to the latrine and discovered the unwelcome person of Ivan at the door. He called my name, and I was so bewildered my "Here, Mein Fuehrer!" stuck in my throat. This mistake brought me a kick from Ivan's pointed boot. I felt a tingling pain like an electric shock for a long time, and hoped, that Ivan had broken his big toe.

This time I was conducted to a different room. Behind the desk sat a Russian major unknown to me. He waved away the guard and spoke in excellent German.

"Please sit down." He indicated a stool near the desk.

"Do you smoke?"

"Yes ... thank you."

The Major also took a cigarette for himself. While we smoked silently, we regarded each other. I nervously sat on the edge of my chair, though this unexpected courtesy threw me completely off guard. The Major made a good impression on me; his face appeared intelligent. The uniform fit him to perfection and was decorated with many medals. This man was undoubtedly a master inquisitor; he picked up a folder and began to question me.

"Your name is Kurt Stock; you are a soldier and belong to Regiment 307 of the 163rd Division. Is that correct?"

"Yes."

"Since you are a soldier, I expect you to address me as 'Herr Major!' "

"Yes, Herr Major."

"Where is your uniform? How is it that you appear before me in civilian clothes?"

I squirmed restlessly on my stool, how could I tell him without arousing suspicion?

The Major appeared to have read my thoughts, and said,

"I should point out to you that whether I believe you or not depends entirely on your answers."

"Our company was dissolved, and we, wandered through the woods in small groups. Driven by extreme hunger, I slipped into a village one night, looking for something to eat. After filling my stomach, I gleaned information about the general situation, and I realized there was no hope of reaching the German lines. Following the advice of the villagers, I put on civilian clothes and expected to wait out the end of the war as a farmhand. I could see no better way out of my desperate situation. I was apprehended in this same village by the Russian commander. The rest you know, Herr Major."

He nodded, stared thoughtfully,

"In what year were you promoted to Lieutenant?" he quizzed.

"Never. My rank is Senior Lance Corporal." I answered directly, and not without some indignation.

Then came his most difficult and unexpected question.

"How many Russian soldiers have you killed?"

"That is very difficult to answer, Herr Major."

"Why?"

"Because I honestly don't know. In battle one follows orders and tries to stay alive. Everybody shoots and the bullets look alike."

"Why didn't you join the *Hitler Jugend?*"

"I had no interest in it, and I wasn't obligated to join."

"In other words, you were against it?"

"At that time, I was too young for any political opinions. I simply was disinterested."

"What are your political views today?"

"Virtually none, Herr Major. I have only one concern —my own welfare."

Without removing his eyes from my face, the Major called the guard.

"You can go now." he said to me, instructing the guard in Russian.

This was the first time I walked back to my cell unaided and without physical pain.

The next one to be questioned was Spiess Kindermann. I whispered quickly, "Stick with the truth."

Peter watched him leave, and when the door closed, he said to me,

"Kurt, if they torture the Spiess like they did before, he's finished!"

I told Peter to relax and told what happened to me. I mentioned that I thought this interrogation was very important.

"I hope your theory is right," Peter commented doubtfully.

"One fact is worth a dozen theories," I said, hopefully.

Kindermann came back, and I was relieved to see that he was not tossed in as usual. He sat down with us, an unfathomable smile on his lips. Peter could not contain his curiosity, and wanted to know immediately, what happened!

The Spiess let Peter dangle on a string while he gave me a surreptitious wink,

"I must say, I've had the most pleasant conversation since I was locked up with you two jailbirds! How nice to speak with an educated man for a change! The courtesy of the Major surpassed ordinary cordiality. He constantly referred to me as 'Herr Captain'. And was quite disappointed when I insisted on remaining Sergeant-Major!".

Peter rolled his eyes while the Spiess asked,

"How did it go with you, Kurt? Were you promoted, too?"

"Only to Lieutenant. I'm sure I'll get my star though, before I leave this place."

Peter had had enough of us and rolled over in the straw, staring at the ceiling. Half to himself, he said,

"Fine buddies I've got. One is a mental case, and the other is merely crazy!"

Kindermann and I grinned.

Around the beginning of May, Ivan appeared right after breakfast with a list. Without any nonsense, he called off seven names; among them were Peter, Kindermann and myself. Before I could exchange a word with Kindermann, we were lined up outside. The Spiess had no opinion about this new maneuver; he merely shrugged his shoulders.

The counting began while we were guarded by a sergeant and five other soldiers. The count was taken several times, and since they arrived at "seven", each time, everything was all right.

"*Choroscho*!"

"*Dawai Marsch*!" was the order and we set off.

Before rounding the corner of the building, I saw Ivan the Terrible for the last time. I said a silent prayer of thanks. He struck his whip playfully against his boots, and gave us a final menacing glare. Then he vanished from my life.

It was a matchless spring morning. If we only knew where we were headed! I tried to talk to Kindermann but a Russian soldier showed me the butt of his rifle, and said,

"*Nix sprrrechen*!"

Everywhere you looked there was ruin and destructions; mountains of broken glass and piles of wrecked furniture were everywhere. Here, lay an empty baby carriage; there, the burned shell of a Panzer tank. German paper money was scattered on the ground like autumn leaves, abundant and worthless.

We ignored the money and often bent to pick up a

cigarette butt. After weaving through the streets of Frankfurt, we came at last to our destination: a prisoner of war camp.

Kindermann, the professional soldier, dug me in the ribs for joy at the sight of numerous soldiers. He said, "Take a good look. Did you ever see anything more beautiful? Just feast your eyes on these genuine assholes, pisspots, *unsoldaten*, and *arschgeigen*!"

Our fate was still in doubt, though. We were civilians and did not belong there. Finally the command of the G.P.U. took precedence over the objections of the watch officer, and the bolt was withdrawn for seven smiling prisoners to march through the gate.

CHAPTER FIVE

The Russian watch officer indicated a soldier to us, who was apparently waiting for our arrival. He wore a spotless, fresh, German uniform. An armband around his left arm read, "*National Kommittee Freies Deutschland*." I looked to Kindermann, wondering if he had an explanation, but he was as ignorant as I was.

The soldier greeted us in a friendly manner but did not explain the nature of his organization. Apparently he was the reception committee; he introduced us to the camp, and told us the itinerary for the next few hours.

"Right away you'll have a haircut, shave and bath."
He looked at our clothes scornfully, then continued in
his thick Rheinish dialect, "Afterwards, you will be given
uniforms to wear. Follow me."

We came to the main street of the camp where one
barrack stood next to the other, as far as the eye could
see. Soldiers stood about idly talking and smoking, in the
beautiful sunshine. What a contrast to the dungeon I had
just left. I was almost happy being back where I belonged.

We came to the bathhouse where we were washed,
brushed, and de-loused. We felt like new men; then we
went to a locker room where we were given new clothing.
Peter looked like a living advertisement for the Luft-
waffe. He smiled happily, and in his eyes shone that
gleam which had faded during the experience with the
G.P.U. Kindermann also looked satisfied; he was given
a Spiess uniform, a sergeant's outfit with two stripes
around the cuffs. I was given an outfit that made me look
like a Christmas tree — odd pieces of clothing. And to
top it all off, I wore one black and one brown shoe!

I inquired among the soldiers waiting for haircuts,
about this "National Komittee". I found out its headquarters was in Moscow, and it was directed by members of the Underground, Pick and Ulbricht. Later I
found out most of these committee people were the
product of a political reorientation. Some of them were
not politically involved at all, but served as interpreters,
police and spies. I did not stay in Frankfurt long enough
to really find out.

After the cleaning operation, which made us feel like
human beings again, we were shown our new barracks.
A Sergeant-Major named Wusthoff was in charge, and
wrote our names into his book. We stood at ease while
he lectured on camp discipline. Everything was organized
in the best German manner. Three times a day there

would be soup and 200 grams of bread, and no more beatings or interrogations! We could profitably use the nights for sleeping. This kind or arrangement met with our unqualified approval.

The camp was divided into groups of one hundred under the supervision of German officers.

I began to feel that I was on furlough, vacationing, rather than in prisoner of war camp.

"Chow time!" It was pea soup with a 200 gram slice of bread which tasted like a five course dinner. Unfortunately, we were still hungry, and for dessert, Kindermann and I smoked a bummed cigarette. As soon as Peter had washed our mess gear, Kindermann suggested,

"Let's disappear! Otherwise they'll put us to work."

We left the barracks right away. Once outside, Kinderman gave us more details. Wusthoff informed Kindermann that the German Commanding Officer believed in a philosophy of keeping soldiers working so that they wouldn't think or worry. Thus, he had drawn up a work plan which was largely concerned with cleaning the barracks and grounds. Kitchen work and latrine duties were special assignments.

That night I slept deeply and undisturbed. The next morning I woke up refreshed and well rested. The day began well — I recognized a sergeant from our batallion staff whom I knew fairly well. In 1942 we were on leave together; he informed me that several of our company had already been transported.

During the day, I talked with many other soldiers. Several had quite an adventure story to tell, just like myself. One question arose in every conversation: What would happen to us? Some were optimistic and believed we would soon be released; but most of us felt certain our next stop would be Siberia.

That night our barracks attended a stage show. It was a variety program, and for two hours I forgot my surroundings. I sat spellbound by the performance. Most of the actors were professionals from the stage, film and radio. The night passed all too quickly; I went to bed happy and full of new hope.

The next day my spirits dropped to zero. Kindermann was being transferred, having been given charge of a barracks. He could not find the right words to say to Peter and me when he left. The soldier in him could not let him show emotions, but finally, he said in his own way,

"Listen, you two assholes! I'll try to transfer you to my barracks as soon as I can."

He looked as if there was something more to say, but we regarded each other, silently. Finally, he tore himself away, turned and walked off without looking back.

As it turned out, there was not enough time to transfer us. The very next day a transport was put together and at 9:00 a.m. we learned that Barracks 31 was among those leaving on it. Everything now moved with great haste. Immediately after breakfast we were all confined to our barracks and around 11:00 a.m. Peter and I joined a long line of prisoners marching out the prison gate. Only the officers and barrack sergeants remained behind. The Russian soldiers who walked beside us now watched us carefully. I saw Kindermann and we exchanged a final greeting. Then I left for an unknown destination.

The loading of the prisoners was done on a side track coming from the main railroad station in Frankfurt. With many a *"Dwai Kamerad"*, and many a *"Job twoju matj"*, (a Russian curse that was much used against us), we were herded like cattle into boxcars. The doors were closed and we found ourselves in complete darkness; the only light and air came from two small barred windows in the top of the boxcar. We lay like sardines packed in a can. After some jolting, the cars rocked and we started rolling. A man watched from the window at the top, and said we were travelling over the Oder Bridge. Then, by the direction of the sun, he judged that we were moving due east.

To escape my nagging hunger, I tried to sleep. Understandably, the air on the lower ledge was impossible to breathe.

"I've got to get out of this!" I thought, making my way over the crumpled bodies to the middle of the car. There the air was a little better.

It was still daylight when we rode into the Polish city of Posen. After the train moved about a bit, it finally came to a full stop. The doors were opened, and we were ordered out. Polish and Russian guards ran about excitedly and the usual counting process began.

After a confused count they concluded that no one was missing. We marched along quickly and soon we came to another prison camp. At the gate we were searched, and admitted in groups of one hundred to an empty area inside the camp, where we were assigned our barracks. Then came registration and a second count, which was even more tedious than the first.

To our general relief, we were given soup. Nothing else happened on this day, the 7th of May 1945. The next day, I discovered many familiar faces from my regiment, even some from my own company. I began to hope I might learn something about Walter and Karl here. I asked everyone about them and found that Walter was right here in the hospital! My long search was at an end. However, Karl was not so lucky; he had been shot on the Baltic.

I ran to the hospital to see Walter. After some searching, I found him in bed. I must have passed him a several times, before I recognized him. I could hardly believe my eyes; he was wasting away with a lung condition. His head was shrunken almost to the size of a small boy's. His eyes caught mine, and his lips twisted into a ghastly smile.

"Hey buddy! I just can't leave you alone for a minute, can I?"

With these — his words — I greeted my friend and comrade-at-arms. He was excited so I patted him on the shoulder, saying,

"Take it easy, Walter. You know that only the good ones die. I know how your concern for your old buddy must have gotten you down — but I made it, didn't I?"

Walter's eyes were wet, and he spoke softly,

"Where the hell have you been keeping yourself, you dumbbell?"

"I'll tell you all about it later, Walter. My time is up and I have to leave now."

Promising to see him the next day — I left.

May 9th was a day not easily forgotten. It is known as the official end of the war. That evening we were given orders to stay in our barracks after the roll call and not venture out. Since we would not be able to use the latrine, we stood up pots and pans for the night. It was understandable why the order was given. The Russians were having a victory celebration and we were not invited. In fact, we sensed that in their happiness, the Russians might take the opportunity to use up all their surplus ammunition in a single night!

Our guess was correct. As soon as it began to get dark, the crack of rifle fire could be heard in the air. There were sounds of wild carousing, bonfires, and shattered glass. Someone shouted "*Hitler Kaput!*". Then a rifle shot. As if on signal, "*Hitler Kaput!*" became the universal cry of the drunken voices, interspersed with rifle shots.

We lay huddled in our cots, miserable. Peace or no peace, a stray bullet at this moment could kill just as before. We were bitter, but not without mixed feelings. We, too, were happy that this stinking war was over. But there was no doubt about it — *they* were the victors!

The barracks was a lonely and dismal place to be with all this ruckus outside. I lay on my side and tried to keep from vomiting, and sleep was a long time in coming. Perhaps tomorrow I could be more objective, I thought, before falling asleep.

CHAPTER SIX

The morning of May 10th was clear and peaceful in more than one sense of the word. The day brought clear skies, streaming sunlight, and pure air. We were not able to forget that we were in prison camp however, especially when we sat down to our delicious fish soup. Every so often fish eyes emerged to the surface and stared up at us, perhaps to wish us a good appetite. I went to the infirmary to inquire about Walter. He was feeling a little better and wanted to know what had happened to me since our fiasco on the Baltic. After I told him my story, he was silent for awhile, then he said dryly,

"Christ! What a bloody trip!"

The orderly gave me a sign indicating that I had to leave. I excused myself from Walter, but promised to return.

Peter awaited me impatiently; he wanted to know everything about Walter. I think he was a bit jealous, but later I realized he had every reason to feel that way. Between my visits to the hospital, I spent most of my time with my old buddies. Naturally, Peter felt slighted. Many times he came along with me but I sensed that he was bored.

The days passed, and nothing unusual happened. There were rumors of a transport, but for the present, nothing definite.

Walter made great strides towards recovery, and I asked if he had heard anything in the hospital about future developments.

"Sure. All they talk about is "transports to the east." he told me.

Then, looking around casually as if to himself, he continued,

"But don't worry, my train goes in the opposite direction."

"That's right, Walter, play it smart. I'm afraid my trip is not over yet. This is just a short stopover."

Afterwards, I saw Peter who told me the most recent rumors. It looked like something was about to happen. A transport would probably be leaving the next day, May 17th.

The rumors materialized, and the next day a transport was put together. Everything in the camp was disrupted. As soon as breakfast was over, I dashed to the infirmary to give Walter the latest news.

"As I said, this was just a stopover. I'm on my way, Walter. Take care of yourself."

Silently, I shook hands with my old pal, and with an effort I tore myself away without looking back — I never saw him again.

Right after lunch we were gathered into columns and marched to the gate. The counting by several Russian officers was very precise and the scenes at Frankfurt were repeated. Shoved and cursed, we were loaded into boxcars. Peter and I stuck together like Siamese twins. I whispered to him,

"Peter, don't forget, we must get a place on the top ledge!"

"Right, Kurt!"

Luck was with us. As soon as the order to enter the boxcars was given, Peter scrambled up into the entrance, agile as a monkey. Then he reached down and pulled me up. From the platform up to the top ledge was a moment's work. Twelve others crowded around us. Each bunk held fourteen men, packed together like peas in a pod, with heads facing the walls. Peter leaned against the wall, and I sat next to him with the window directly above us. Since there were four ledges, two on each side, holding fourteen men apiece, there were fifty-six men altogether in the boxcar. The door rolled shut; then we heard an iron bar being drawn into position.

The train still did not move for awhile, and I regarded my new travelling companions with curiosity. Not a familiar face in the whole lot. However, I would get to know them well before the trip was over.

Directly opposite me lay a mountain of a man whose big frame took up room for two. His sweaty feet were right under my arm pit. His name was Wilhelm Potscra who was born and raised on a farm in east Prussia. Everything about him was big, from his nose to his feet — and his hands were the size of dinner plates.

Right next to him, sat a character as contrasting in size and weight as one could imagine. He was a Saxon from Dresden, who, because of his mousy appearance — a small face, pointed teeth and pale lips, was named "Mouse" immediately by Wilhelm.

Then there was Ludwig, our witty raconteur. He hailed from Bonn. His face was always smiling, and his mouth was never closed. He was a natural comedian who had a bag of jokes that was bigger than a department store. Next to him lay Otto Becker — he was a unique type, a true product of Berlin; he possessed a big mouth, but a heart of gold. He had a finger in every pie — a real operator, show-off, and organizer. Otto could get away with the impossible. For example: It is a well known fact that the Russians had an inordinate fondness for watches, which they stole whenever they could. However, they never got to see Otto's. He carried his wrist watch and diamond ring all the way to Siberia by carving a hole in his bread ration, and placing the ring and watch inside; then he kneaded the wet dough until it resembled an ordinary piece of bread. In all our years as prisoners, the Russians conducted many surprise raids, but they never touched a man's bread ration. Naturally, he replaced the bread often, never allowing it to go stale.

We all were convinced that nothing could surprise us any more, but we were wrong. Otto astonished all of us on the ledge by producing a whole bag of tobacco. This won him instant admiration from everyone. He began slowly rolling a cigarette while our envious eyes were glued to him. He looked around pityingly, saying,

"My source of supply has been temporarily interrupted. This stuff is a skillful blend of tobaccos from many countries, and the price is climbing rapidly."

He took a long drag, chuckled, and said,

"Ah! That's what I call tobacco! I'm going to order a wagon load of this as soon as we get to Moscow."

I decided to give him a chance to save his life before we all robbed him:

"If you ever expect to sell that dried horse-shit, you'd better let us sample it first."

Otto was clever enough not to push his luck too far.

"My good sirs," he said, objectively, "This is your first and last sample. Each man gets one cigarette. But," he raised his finger, "Only a small one!"

Otto passed the tobacco around, peering carefully to make sure that no one took too much. Thus, the situation was saved, and everyone was satisfied.

"You were just speaking of horse-shit," Ludwig said, "That reminds me of a joke I heard back home . . ."

Ludwig did not have time to finish; the door opened and a Russian officer looked into the doorway. He was accompanied by several soldiers, and compared the population of the boxcar with a list. In a brittle German accent, he asked if anyone spoke Russian. Peter was going to answer, but Wilhelm spoke up before him. "I do." he said, stepping down. He and the officer began an incomprehensible conversation.

Finally, Wilhelm turned around, explaining, "The transport officer has put me in charge of this boxcar. I'm responsible for keeping order here. He also said that we're going to be together for sme time. If we show him cooperation, then he in turn will do everything for us that he can."

The officer appeared to be pleased with the translation. He said, *"Choroscho"*, and the door closed. Wilhelm remained standing in the centre of the boxcar, looking like a giant among dwarfs.

"Listen to me," his voice droned, "You are all witnesses to the thankless position I'm in. I'll try my best to make everything run as smoothly as possible. Since I am in charge, I will not tolerate any one acting out of place. My name is Wilhelm Potschka, and if anyone has anything to say, I would like to hear it now."

Wilhelm looked around challengingly; while our silence gave him the approval he needed for leadership.

By Otto's watch it was 6:00 p.m., and we still were not moving. We speculated on whether we would eat before we moved off. Around seven we heard noises outside. Looking through the bars of the car window I relayed the information to the others — food was on the way. In minutes, the door was opened, and Wilhelm received the mess.

First came the dry bread, then two pails of hot pea soup and one of thin coffee. The rationing was carried out properly and without commotion. Certainly it was hardly enough to satisfy our stomachs, but we were content; we had known far worse. From the five slices of bread I received, I ate three immediately. I felt that our next meal lay somewhere in the distant future. The sun had set, and darkness lay over the land like a thick blanket. Nothing more could be seen, while outside was the noise and bustle of a train station. Most of the prisoners in the boxcar were quiet. Only Ludwig was heard. For dessert, he provided us with some of his dirty jokes.

Otto's neighbor, the Mouse from Dresden, asked, "Why don't you sex maniacs shut up? I'm trying to get some sleep!"

Ludwig did not have the opportunity to answer because the train began to rock back and forth, and with a jolt, we set off. A shrill locomotive whistle was our farewell message.

I knelt before the airhole trying to see; the lights danced in rows, faster and faster. After a while, as the train picked up speed, they disappeared into the darkness. In the boxcar everything was peaceful; even Ludwig was quiet because no one listened to his jokes anymore. The wheels rattled out a monotonous song.

The next day we were deep in Polish territory and the journey continued as if there was not a moment to lose. We discussed our possible destination, and no matter how much we tried to delude ourselves, "Siberia" was in our thoughts all the time.

In the morning, we passed through many villages and small cities, but we moved so quickly that I could not make out their names. The train finally stopped at Kutnow, and as soon as the door was opened Wilhelm received his new orders.

"It says," Wilhelm translated, "We are going to leave the boxcar for some fresh air and to stretch our limbs. We must move around in a circle, and the guards will shoot anyone who attempts to break it."

"When do we eat?" Mouse asked.

"Come on — let's get out of here!" was Wilhelm's answer.

Spurred on by many a *"Dawai!"* and *"Job twoju matj!"* we did our morning exercises. Then we were hustled back to the boxcar. After two hours we began moving again.

Most of us had saved a piece of dry bread which we chewed on, but it made our powerful thirst much worse. Otto rolled himself a cigarette; and every eye followed

the smoke, which moved around in strange patterns. I
was the first to reach the butt. Around midday, the
boxcar had become like a hot oven and our thirst by now
was excruciating. Even Ludwig was quiet, without any
inspiration to joke.

Finally, the train stopped at 2:00 in the afternoon.
From the commotion, we knew we were finally going to
eat. Our boxcar was opened and Wilhelm went into action.
The soup was thin and meagre; the bread fresh and soggy.
The most welcome part of the meal was two pails of water,
and for the first time, fighting broke out between two
prisoners. In the struggle, one of the pails spilled; curses
ensued, while accusations were thrown back and forth.

Wilhelm stepped right into the middle of the dispute,
immediately demonstrating that he did not intend to treat
the culprits with kid gloves. Using his mighty hands, he
grabbed one with his right and the other with his left!
They squirmed like snakes while he pushed them both
against the wall and held them there. He ordered,

"You will stay here until I finish giving out the rations.
I will not tolerate any fighting."

And as if nothing had happened, Wilhelm calmly
continued dividing the rations. His manner was subdued,
and his voice controlled as he inquired,

"What was the reason for the commotion?"

Both men tried to speak at once, but with a wave of
his right hand, which looked like a flying dinner plate, he
ordered them to be quiet.

"You first!" he said, poking his index finger at one
of them.

Wilhelm listened carefully as a judge of his excuse,
and when he finished Wilhelm approached the other,
"Now let's hear from you!"

The other soldier sputtered out his account, leaving
Wilhelm with the final word. He scratched his unshaven
chin, deep in thought. He was going to make the best of
the situation and every eye was viewing him critically. Here

was the chance to demonstrate his leadership qualities.

In my opinion, Wilhelm's decision was very good; the wisdom of Solomon was in it. He said something to this effect:

"No doubt about it, this is one hell of a situation. There is only one portion of water left in the pail. You two have another one: but there are three of us." He took the water from the one man and poured it back into the pail. "Well, the only thing we can do now is to make three portions out of two."

The prisoners appeared satisfied with this arrangement. Also, Wilhelm had very cleverly settled all doubts about his right to leadership.

Minutes later our prison on wheels began moving again, and it was seven p.m. when we came to the outskirts of Warsaw. As we waited, we realized that our evening meal wouldn't be forthcoming.

Civilians stood about, trying to come close to our cars, but were held off by the guards. They shook their fists at us, shouted and threw stones.

A teenaged boy worked himself close to the car, and suddenly pulling out a sling-shot, began to fire at us. The stones came too close for comfort, hitting the bars of the window. We took cover, and none too soon at that! A stone the size of a pigeon's egg found its way through the window, hitting the opposite wall of the boxcar. Otto remarked dryly,

"I'd give half my tobacco for a gun with one round of ammunition!"

As no further objects came flying in our direction, I dared glance through the window, seeing a Russian soldier chasing the teenager away by waving his gun.

"You can lift your head up again, Otto!" I said. "William Tell has been routed."

The train rocked again, and soon we were on our way, travelling until about three in the morning. The train stopped and was pulled off to a side-track where nothing happened for the time being.

Since it appeared we weren't going to get anything to eat here, too, we went back to sleep.

Around six in the morning, the door was opened, and a group of Polish and Russian officers stood outside. Apparently we had reached the Polish-Russian border. We were ordered to leave the car and lined up in rows of five. As soon as the last man had descended, the officers climbed aboard and searched it inch by inch.

In the meantime, we were counted several times, and checked against the transport list. One prisoner received a terrible blow with a rifle butt, because during the counting he relieved his bladder. The Russians got furious over any disturbance during their concentrated counting!

(Later, in Siberia, I was punished for a similar offence. During the counting of our brigade, I turned around for a cigarette light; at first the counting Tartar cursed me, but when he realized he had forgotten his count, he really got angry. All I remember seeing was the white of his slanted eyes, and after he was through with me I sustained a few sore ribs and a beautiful shiner on my right eye.)

At last the customs inspection was over and the train was rerouted to the main track, which we rode into Brest-Litovsk. Over the bustle of the busy railroad station we heard, with welltrained ears, the noise of the food delivery.

To our astonishment, they gave us a larger supply of bread than usual. Then came the catch — it was supposed to last for two days! They also gave us more water. Peter and I put one ration of bread in reserve. Then we were let out of the car to walk around in a circle, exercising for fifteen minutes.

The sun was high in the heavens when we began our journey again. The next big city we stopped at was Minsk. We were given enough time to relieve our bladders, and were off again. The heat in the car was murderous and fighting broke out frequently.

Wilhelm really had his hands full trying to keep order. Everyday he complained about excruciating pains in his gut. He was often doubled over with the pain. Sometimes he gave away his food in exchange for cigarettes. He was still boney and big but it was obvious to all of us that Wilhelm was seriously ill. Now he was reduced to pleading with us instead of commanding.

Mouse and Peter on the other hand, stood the ordeal fairly well. Otto was stingier than ever with his tobacco. Sometimes, it appeared he would rather burn his finger-nails than relinquish his butt. Even Ludwig had run out of wit; I felt, though, he had burned all his fire works in the first few days.

Peter remained calm; he was a good comrade and friend. I noticed that the blond hair on his chin was beginning to grow, and some of the others already had the makings of formidable beards.

Hunger was our first concern. Undernourishment, stale bread, and the cramped posture in which we spent most of the day was responsible for a great deal of wind-breaking. Now I was happier than ever with my place near the boxcar window.

The train progressed through Orscha and on to Smolensk, where we were given something to eat at last. This stop-over lasted two days and nights, and we lay around the boxcar, dirty, hungry, and demoralized. We became stuporous and indifferent .as though we had lost our spirit. Yet, despite our poor condition, the beauty of the Russian churches and countryside was appreciated by quite number of us.

After two full days of stop-over, we moved full steam ahead, heading straight for Moscow. We asked ourselves if the capital of the Soviet Union was our final destination? Otto's opinion was that this would be excellent from a business point of view. He was almost going crazy from his inability to transact business while he was couped up inside the boxcar. However, he kept an eye out for the future, using the time in the boxcar to learn as many Russian words and expressions as he could from Wilhelm. He asked endless questions, and naturally, Wilhelm always had first chance for his cigarette butts.

I also tried to learn Russian. With the help of Peter, I took my first steps into the Russian language. We reached Moscow at night.

The city was brightly lit; the Moscow night life was in full swing. In the grey light of morning we sat around waiting. Finally, around seven o'clock we heard the familiar sound of food being delivered. Again we were given bread for two days and we realized that we had not yet reached our destination. Indeed, right after breakfast, we began our journey again. Siberia came closer. After two more days of travelling, we came to Saransk; then, on the following day, to Kubysow. It was raining; the heavens had pitied us. It poured all day, cooling off the hot air.

Our thoughts were concentrated on our hunger; there was no room for anything else. On our bunk lay a calm and not particularly distinguished Hanoverian whose name was Heini Kuhnert. By trade he was a cook and often during the transport he would give us samples of his knowledge. Occasionally, we would ask him to bake us a cake or cook us a hearty meal. Heini went through the preliminaries, as we lay back in preparation for the feast. Mentally, we ate the most appetizing delicacies, cakes, sauces, and soups. Heini was a real master. In no time at all, our minds were in paradise, while our stomachs were in hell.

Otto still had some tobacco left, but he had run out of matches. Heini, the chef, swapped him two matches for one cigarette. Shortly afterwards, Otto asked for another match. Heini asked for one match for half a cigarette. Otto smoked, grumbling quietly for a while, then commented,

"Heini, you are the worst tobacco thief I ever met."

"Ha! Look who is talking now. The master wheeler and dealer himself!"

Otto carped: "Alright, alright — give me the match!"

From now on, we noticed that Otto rolled his cigarettes mighty thin.

In the late afternoon, the rain stopped, the heavens lit up and the sun came out. It wouldn't be long before we were given something to eat. The Russian supply crew stepped through the mud, and with much cursing and spitting, forwarded the steaming bucket of soup. Thank God we did not stay here longer than necessary. As soon as we were fed, the train began to move again.

That night we witnessed a beautiful sunset. One must be a poet to describe its beauty. The colors spread across the heavens reminded me of Norway, the land of the midnight sun. There too, I had been moved by the gorgeous panorama of the dying sun.

The train came to the Urals, and Ludwig, our human joke book, was again the object of attention. He was now undisputed farting champion. The Mouse from Dresden could only emit a few whining puffs now.

Our next stop was Ufa, here we had the opportunity to stretch our legs. The difference was immediately apparent. At the beginning of the journey, we would jump in and out of the boxcar like playful monkeys. Now we moved like invalids, stumbling around in a circle. Our clothes hung loosely on our emaciated limbs and with empty eyes we looked silently to the east, as if there lay the answers to all our questions.

Climbing back into the boxcar we must have been a pitiful sight. Some prisoners were so weak, they hung on to the arms of their comrades like sacks of potatoes. I was never near the end of my rope. Some of us were seriously ill. Wilhelm's health was sinking rapidly; the wet, sour bread caused him great stomach pain; sometimes, he gave part of his soup to Mouse.

At last the journey began again, and we passed over

the Urals in a single night. The sun had already reached its highest point when we rode into Tscheljabinsk, a fairly large city. We waited, longingly, for the noise of the food delivery, but nothing was heard. From the window, I saw many soldiers running about, shouting, cursing, and filled with excitement. Intuitively, I felt something special was going on down there.

CHAPTER SEVEN

We soon found out what it was all about when the doors opened and the wild, half-starved beasts were unloaded from the cage. The command was given to take our possessions with us as we left the car.

Were we finally at our destination? The Russians seemed to be full of vigor and boundless enthusiasm. As they liberally dispensed curses and rifle blows. Several prisoners were very sick and were loaded onto a truck. Others who were too weak to stand on their feet were brutally forced up by the guards. We were counted, and after this last torment, we began moving at last while the guards snapped at us like dogs bringing in sheep.

Several Russian officers watched the long line of half-starved prisoners walking up the road, while smoking factory chimneys and shrill sirens bid us grim welcome. With sagging stomachs and rubber knees, the "Rehabilitation Brigade" stumbled forward.

As we moved along in this wretched condition, we received another kind of welcome from the civilian population.

One man cried, "The German pigs are here!"

Another shook his fist and greeted us triumphantly, *"Hitler Kaput!"*

The Russian language does not have the sound "h". Instead they say "g"; thus "Gitler — Gimmler," etc. One of the prisoners was named Heinrich Hochhausen — they really had fun with his name!

A man wearing an inspector's uniform walked beside us. He spoke German with a strong accent. His words of greeting were,

"Welcome to Dachau, *mein Herren.*"

Most of the civilians regarded us as if we were from another planet. Afterwards, I heard about a woman who had been astonished by our appearance. She believed that all Germans had two horns and a tail — like the Devil.

Although I did not experience it myself, I was told later of certain degradations that took place in Moscow. After going without food for a long time, the German prisoners were given a good meal containing much fat. Afterwards, they were led through the streets of Moscow. The fat did not stay well in the stomach. Hardly any of the prisoners could restrain their bowels, and they sat down and defecated, regardless of where they were. To the civilians it was evident that these prisoners, and therefore all Germans, were, no better than pigs. It was a propaganda trick that worked perfectly.

Finally, we stood before the gate of the prison. When the painful ordeal of counting, arguing, and other red tape was finished, I was able to take a look at my new home.

Over the camp gate was an enormous stone wreath — a sickle and hammer in its center. Peter translated the inscription around the wreath: "He who does not work, shall not eat." In the coming years it was to become clear that these were not empty words. It was, in fact, the slogan of the Russians.

A high wooden palisade garnished with barbed wire

ran around the camp. The large gate was opened and with the cry *"Dawai Marsch"*, we entered Prison Camp 6/10 of Tscheljabinsk. We were greeted by Major Bogoslaw, the Russian camp commander. I could not understand much of what he said but he seemed angry about something. After he had finished speaking, the German camp leader, Spiess Wiegand, translated.

Wiegand concluded his remarks in the manner typical of a sergeant, saying,

"The Major would like to stress that you are not here on a vacation; you are here to rebuild Russia. He who works diligently, will receive enough to eat. Order, Sobriety and Discipline are my department, and I assure you, that I will put a fire under anyone who steps out of line and creates a disturbance."

We were assigned to our barracks. Fortunately our entire group from the boxcar was assigned to the same place. Only the roof of the barracks was visible. We later learned, there was a reason for this unusual mode of construction. Two-thirds of the barracks are built underground, and therefore, well protected from the wind and cold.

We had to descend some stairs to enter our new quarters. Everything was plain, and dilapidated. In general, what we saw was ugly and at the same time, manifestly practical. I saw this often in Russia; they are a practical, no-nonsense people. Here is a story which travelled from camp to camp;

A german prisoner, an electrician, had a love affair with a Russian woman, while they were working on the nightshift of a factory. The woman became pregnant and gave birth to twins. Under pressure she named the father, and the whole matter was taken to a Russian judge, who asked the prisoner,

"Do you admit that you are the father of these two children?"

"Yes."

"Would you mind telling me how you intend to provide for them?"

"As a prisoner of war, it would be difficult but as an electrician, I could."

"In other words, as a free man you could?"

"Yes, your Honor, indeed I could!"

"Very well. You'll have an opportunity to prove it."

The prisoner of war was released and allowed to work as a "free" man in the same factory as the woman. He was driven by the same "norm-devil", and geographically his situation had not changed much either, neither was free to leave Siberia (The Russians have a simple view of life.)

Alfred Krauskopf, barracks sergeant of Barracks No. 8, outlined our itinerary for the rest of the day. He had a shrill, jarring voice and screeched that we would have something to eat later, and now he was ready to answer any of our questions.

Peter winced.

"Do you have a cramp?" I asked.

"That man's voice is giving me goose pimples," Peter explained, as the hair stood up on his arms.

"That jackass has a voice like a eunuch." Ludwig added.

Otto said, "It seems to me the service in this hotel is not to my taste. I don't think they maintain this whorehouse very well. I intend to move out as soon as possible."

Defiantly, he sat down on the bare wood, while Mouse sat cross-legged like a tailor, nodding silently. Dejectedly, he said,

"I come from a good family, and this is below my standards."

Wilhelm and the cook from Hanover lay on their backs staring silently at the ceiling when a messenger appeared in the doorway, announcing,

"Barracks 8 is going to chow!"

These magic words brought the prisoners back to life,

and we grabbed our pots and hurried off to the kitchen. After eating, they sent the first group off to the delousing station. When they came back, we could hardly believe our eyes. Every one was shaved bald. Naturally, there was much joking about this; we laughed heartily. After a few hours when we were in line ourselves, the smiles faded. Our convict haircuts were not a joking matter any more. But after we had bathed, we felt better.

Next day, a complaint was sent to the Russian commander about our scalping. Major Bogoslaw informed us that all Russian soldiers had their heads shaven, and what was good enough for them was good enough for us. Besides, he did not understand why we were complaining.

After a few days at the camp, we saw no more reason for complaint, either. It was another example of the homely Russian way of doing things. The problem was mainly head lice, while bedbugs and fleas were the other bloodsuckers that plagued us day and night. Our barracks, and all other buildings in the camp, were natural incubators for these parasites. Only three weeks after our arrival, I killed my first hundred lice. The bedbugs did not treat me too badly; perhaps I did not have their blood group. But Peter suffered enormously from them.

Fleas were more difficult to deal with. Also, mice and rats found a comfortable home inside the barracks. What they lived on is a mystery; they certainly couldn't get anything from me. Mainly through, the worst enemies of the prisoner were hunger, the Siberian winter, and homesickness. Of the numerous diseases that festered in the camp, I will speak of later.

The next day we were called for a medical examination. It was an important day, and would decide our future camp life.

Because of its importance, all the Russian camp officers were present. Wiegand, the German camp commander, was of course, there too. In the middle of this assembly stood the Russian doctor, Lidia Novotnik. She seemed very sure of her position, doing all the talking, and making most of the decisions. She examined each prisoner with merciless eyes which crept over every inch of our bodies. Her pale, uncurved lips gave her face an imperious, cynical quality. I immediately disliked her. Yet, her Asiatic features possessed an icy, Oriental beauty.

"Ludwig Tietze."

Ludwig was the first on the list. He removed his clothing and stood before the Novotnik. Her unfriendly eyes crept over Ludwig's emaciated body.

In a hard German, she asked, "Healthy?"

"Stomach pains!"

What's wrong with it?"

"Always hungry!" came the prompt answer.

Ludwig waved his arms, and we jabbed one another in the ribs. That's telling her! The doctor seemed not to see him.

"Turn around!" she barked.

Her lips were as straight as a knife. Playing impatiently with her pen, she ordered him to come closer. With practiced fingers she felt the muscles of Ludwig's rear end. Finally she decided to put him in Group Two which meant eight hours work in heavy industry. It was later evident that Ludwig was lucky.

If his rear end muscles had been just a bit stronger, she would have classified him in Group One. That meant ten hours work, in the coal or lead mines.

The next was the Dresden Mouse.

"Healthy?"

"Yes."

"Turn around."

The Novotnik looked coldly at the poorly-built Mouse. Lieutenant Burgajeff, the Russian work-officer, spoke to the doctor who listened, then said, decisively, "Nyet!"

Mouse was put in Group 3-6. This meant working for only six hours. Generally, this involved unloading trucks, grounds maintenance, or road repair work. After a few others had been examined, it was Otto's turn.

Lidia Novotnik looked Otto up and down, then called Burgajeff over. They talked for awhile, and finally he said, *"Choroscho."*

She turned back to Otto.

"Healthy?"

"Yes."

'Very well. You can go."

Otto Becker, the Berlin operator, was given a job that well-suited his activities. He was assigned to the camp supply crew which loaded and unloaded provisions by trucks. It was ideal for his conniving nature. Otto was one of those people who always seems to land on his feet, no matter where you drop him, even in a prison camp.

The next was Wilhelm, our boxcar leader. When asked about his health, he told of terrible pains in his stomach. The doctor's eyes narrowed.

"How long have you had this pain?"

"Maybe six months." he answered.

"Turn around!" came the order.

Novotnik discussed Wilhelm with Lieutenant Burgajeff. They debated for some time, when Major Bogoslaw became interested and entered the conversation. Finally, the doctor stood up and walked over to Wilhelm. Like a professor lecturing to some medical students, she demonstrated her arguments on Wilhelm's rear. I could not understand the discussion; but this much was clear. Wilhelm's sagging buttocks were not satisfactory. The appearance of his behind contrasted sadly with his mighty build, it looked like the lifeless breasts of an old woman.

The Novotnik returned to her table, and wrote for a while. That day Wilhelm was sent to the hospital.

Peter and I went into Group Two because one of my war wounds lay near my spine. I berated myself for not attempting to lower my classification by one group.

Another one of us had luck that day. Heini Kuhnert,

the cook from Hanover, was made a cook in the camp kitchen. Later, because of his exceptional skill, he was put in charge of all the hospital food. The hospital sick were given smaller quantities, better quality food. Instead of 600 grams of black bread, patients were given 400 grams of white bread.

The prison resembled the army in many ways — men were thrown together and torn apart again. Friendships developed quickly in moments of anguish and danger. On the other hand, the lowest aspects of human nature rose to the surface, too, — the cowards, spies, informers, turncoats, and others who formed a class by themselves. I will have more to say about these individuals later.

Our first day in the camp passed without incident. Brigades were formed to clean the barracks. Wilhelm said goodbye before going to the hospital, and we all promised to visit as soon as possible. Mouse was moved to Barracks 12. Otto Becker and Heini Kuhnert, because their work was directly connected with the camp administration, moved into Barracks 25, where the "middle class" lived. The German camp commander, Sergeant Wiegand, had a room all to himself at the camp — for these people, hunger was rarely a problem.

Ludwig, Peter and I were still together in Barracks 8. We decided to take a good look around our new home, and my first impression of Camp 6-10 was that it was very dirty, poorly maintained and unsanitary. Equipment fell apart at the touch. As we wandered down the main road of the camp, we came to what was apparently the central core. Here were the kitchen, hospital and dentist's offices, while farther along we came to the shoe and clothing dispensaries. Walking a little more, we reached the edge of the camp. Before us lay the "sepretnaja sona", the danger zone. Peter stood too close to the wire, and excited the watch guard.

"*Nazat job twoju matj, nazat!*", he cried, raising his

automatic to firing position. We turned back at once. Continuing our investigation in another direction, we came to the latrines and stopped to relieve ourselves. What we saw here was beneath the dignity of man. The latrine was a wide trench with boards crossed over it, leaving holes over which a man could squat. The stench was unbearable, and the flies bestial.

Since Russian newspapers were used to roll cigarettes, there was a shortage of paper in the camp. Truthfully, we used anything we could find, grass, stones, wood, etc., to wipe ourselves. I am convinced that if I had had a supply of toilet paper, it would have netted me a small fortune. There were prisoners with dysentery who sat over this hole for hours, while others with diarrhoea or weak bladders also spent much time there. In our barracks alone, there were many unfortunates who went to the latrine as much as ten times a night.

After the evening meal, the whole camp amassed together for the *powerka,* the evening roll call. This *powerka* was of great importance, but since each count always came up with a different number, the drama usually turned into a ludicrous comedy. Spiess Wiegand tried to systematize the counting, but he was unsuccessful. Somehow, though, the right answer appeared, and we were dismissed.

I will not mention these *powerkas* any more than necessary, but I can only say they were long, drawn-out, and exasperating. They did become slightly more tolerable as time went on.

I discovered that there were many prisoners in this camp from other countries — Hungarians, Bulgarians, Rumanians, and others. There was a rumor, which was confirmed, that all nationalities except the Germans and Austrians would soon be leaving. This did not please the Austrians at all, but when only Germans and Austrians remained, Spiess Wiegand was able to demonstrate his leadership qualities. His military voice was loud and clear, and his orders precise. There was no difficulty in executing his commands: When Spiess Wiegand was put in charge of the count, he always did it quickly, reporting the figures to Major Bogoslaw. His count was always correct, and the Russian's *"job twoju matj"* expressed real surprise.

After the roll call, Ludwig, Peter and I went to Barracks 25 searching for Otto. It was unbelievable; his tobacoo pouch was filled up again. Politely, he offered Ludwig and me a smoke; in return we did not ask him any impertinent questions. Otto described his situation — here in Barracks 25 were the tradesmen or officials of the camp. This was essential for conducting business, he said.

"Remember where you come from, and don't talk so big." I reprimanded him.

Heini helped himself to a cigarette and we sat around smoking. Then Otto asked,

"Have you heard the latest shit-house talk?"

We looked at him for further information.

"A large transport of German soldiers is coming, including officers."

"That's quite possible," Ludwig said, "Since our allies have to leave."

"I have more news to report, too." Otto continued.

"You're a real news agency." I said, but from the way Otto regarded me, I knew I had smoked my last cigarette for the evening.

"About two miles from here there's a large truck factory; you can hear the noise here, and three-hundred and fifty men from the camp are going to be put to work there. From what I have heard, the work is dangerous, dirty, and hard."

"We'll find out soon enough." I said.

Spiess Wiegand entered the barracks, going directly to his room. This man was all personality; he was the only man in Barracks 25 who had a room all to himself. His personal messenger and lackey slept like a watchdog outside his room.

It was getting late; we wished Otto good night and hurried back to our barracks. It was still fairly dark when Krauskopf sounded the alarm for breakfast next morning. Still half asleep, we slurped the sour *Kapusta* soup (cabbage soup). We later learned why we were awakened so early — the cooks had to prepare meals for 1368 men, and the kitchen needed the kettles for the next meal. Feeding such a number took hours, and today we were the first shift.

Krauskopf howled at us; his shrill voice and the sour cabbage soup blended perfectly together.

Two prisoners began to insult one another furiously; each accused the other of unfairly dividing the bread. Onion-head Krauskopf spoke of a barracks' cleaning, making us realize it was high time to leave. As inconspicuously as possible, the three of us slipped out the door. The fresh air made us realize how unhealthy and congested it really was inside the barracks.

We went to the latrine, but the news agency was not yet in operation. Our next stop was around the kitchen, the international stamping grounds. All kinds of trading was conducted here.

Shortly after we arrived, Ludwig had his first bid. A Hungarian confessed an interest in Ludwig's boots, and offered him ten rubles, two packs of Machorka, half a newspaper, and his old boots in trade. Ludwig did not know what to do.

I advised him to wait, "You can get a better deal than that!"

After leaving the Hungarian standing there, we walked away slowly. I ran into a buddy from my own company who had just traded his army sweater for tobacco. I congratulated him, and he gave me a cigarette.

We did not have to wait long before the Hungarian returned.

"Comrade," he said, "I'll give you fifteen rubles and

three hundred grams of bread in addition to everything else I promised you."

Ludwig regarded Mr. Paprika's shoes, and turning to me indecisively, he said,

"They appear as though he made the whole trip from Hungary to Siberia on foot!" I offered Ludwig the rest of my cigarette which he pushed aside, saying to the Hungarian, "Make that six hundred grams of bread and they're yours."

The Magyar thought for a while, then said, "Agreed." The deal was completed behind a building. When Ludwig later found ou the value of a ruble, he was ready to strangle the Hungarian — a pound of sugar cost 35 rubles.

I went to see Wilhelm while Ludwig and Peter went off the find Mouse.

The hospital had two German doctors on its staff. Chief Surgeon, Karl-Gunter Meinicke, was the principal one and his assistant was Dr. Ferdinand Lubke. These doctors devoted endless hours caring for the sick and injured. Dr. Meinicke had earned himself a reputation during the war as a performer of surgical miracles behind the front line. His skill did not fail him even under direct fire, and many owed their lives to his knowledge and masterful scalpel.

The Russians tied his skillful hands completely, despite all that he tried to do for the camp. Lidia Novotnik never let the German doctors forget that she was the one in charge of the hospital. She frequently contradicted his diagnoses and dismissed many sick patients as malingerers. Serious cases that required immediate surgery were kept waiting, and the death rate in the camp from 1945 to 1947 reached epidemic proportions. Ultimately, even Moscow was disturbed and sent an investigation committee.

On two points, one couldn't complain about Lidia Novotnik — they were order and cleanliness. She wandered through the bedrows, running her finger through the most remote corners, looking for dust. Naturally, it was not long before the Novotnik was feared and hated by everyone in the camp and it became increasingly difficult for Doctor Meinicke to maintain his dignity and conceal his deep disgust for the Novotnik.

I obtained permission to visit Wilhelm and it was good to see a real smile on his face. I told him all the latest rumors,

"Ludwig sold his shoes and sends you some tobacco."

Wilhem was touched by the gift and rolled himself a cigarette. I looked him over and became disheartened; Wilhelm was seriously ill.

"How do you feel, Wilhelm? Have they done anything to help you?"

"Meinicke examined me yesterday, but he didn't cheer me any. He spoke of an x-ray before he could make an accurate diagnosis."

The end of my visiting hour came, and I had to say good-bye to Wilhelm. I promised to see him again and shook his hand emotionally.

I found my comrades lying behind the barracks in the grass and I told them about Wilhelm, saying he would like visitors. Mouse promised to visit him the next morning.

Later in the afternoon, a messenger ran through all the barracks calling for all prisoners who spoke Russian. The messenger could give no further information, except that they were to report to Barracks 21, the Administration Building.

I encouraged Peter to go. There were about a dozen altogether who answered the call. They came out, singly from the barracks, and finally Peter returned.

"You'll never guess what's happened to me!" he said.

"Well, tell me!"

"The Russians are looking for two men who can read and write Russian. Their responsibilities will be office work, messenger service, and administrative duties connected with the working brigades."

"And?"

"I'm one of the two. What do you think of that, Kurt?"

"I don't know; it could mean all kinds of advantages. You'll be able to pass on useful information to Ludwig and me, also, you won't have to do heavy labor, and most importantly, you'll have protection."

"But," Peter continued, "What are the disadvantages?"

"You can only find that out for yourself. It's useless to speculate. Just be careful and watch out for tricks. They're going to test you."

"Perhaps I'm too inexperienced, Kurt."

"It's too late now. Tell me, what's next?"

"I'm moving into Barracks 25 to await further orders."

"What more do you want?" I tried to joke, "You now belong to high society!"

"Very funny!" said Peter, sarcastically.

We found an unoccupied place and sat down on the grass. Resting on my elbow, I watched camp activity feeling that Peter still had something more to say. After a while he asked,

"Kurt?"

"Hm?"

Peter was searching for the right words.

"We've been together since we went to prison, and you're the only real friend I have."

He still was unsatisfied because he had not expressed himself exactly as he wanted to.

"Don't worry, Peter," I said, "We won't be far apart, and we'll see each other as often as possible. Nothing's changed between us. Right?"

"Right!" Peter smiled, feeling better.

"Come." I said, "Let's hurry and tell Ludwig the good news."

We found him sleeping on his bunk. I grabbed his nose, and he awakened with a start, gasping for breath.

"Hey, Lazybones, Peter's leaving us."

Ludwig yawned sleepily, and hardly moving, asked,

"Home leave or a short vacation on the Krim?"

"Something like that. But first he's moving to Barracks 25 to wait for his travelling papers to be signed."

Peter explained what had happened to him, while Ludwig shook his head in disbelief.

"Tell me, Kurt. Why is it that everyone we know elevates himself, except for you and me? Are we so stupid?"

We congratulated Peter some more, and all three of us went to Barracks 25 to see Heini and Otto. Otto said that he had inside knowledge that the other nationalities would be leaving tomorrow, and the day afterwards, the expected transport of German soldiers would be arriving.

He was right; the next day our former allies were ready to leave camp. One saw many smiling faces who believed that they were going back home. Ludwig stood next to me, whispering,

"If they're going home, I'll eat these chewed up clodhoppers!"

As if springing out of the earth, the Hungarian suddenly stood before us.

"Comrade!" he said, "Here! Take this *katusha*. I won't need it in Hungary; we have matches there!"

Before Ludwig could say a word, he was gone! Ludwig looked at his present, shaking his head. In his hand, he held three separate items, a piece of steel, grindstone, and what appeared to be a wick placed inside a three inch long tube.

It took us a while to figure out how it worked. In principle the apparatus was very simple; the wick was ignited by striking a spark from the steel file and grindstone, and it glowed as long as it was outside the pipe. When it was pulled back, the ember went out instantly. However, the black ash that accumulated on the end of the wick made it receptive to the next spark.

We eventually succeeded in making it work and Ludwig put his *katusha* into his pocket. Then he looked down at his floppy shoes, and rocked back and forth in them, saying,

"You know, Kurt? These shoes aren't half as bad as I thought."

As soon as the last of our allies had marched through the camp gate, things started moving again. Peter was called to the work office and soon he was dashing from barracks to barracks. He had only enough time to tell me that the work brigades were being assembled. The "Black Brigade" of 300 men would leave tomorrow morning and at noon time Ludwig and I learned that we were included.

The Black Brigade was composed of those who lived in Barracks 8, 9 and 10. We were assembled together by three brigadiers who all spoke Russian, and were also prisoners of war like ourselves. The first brigade, composed of 200 men, worked in the various shops while the rest worked outside, clearing roads, digging ditches, and piling up scrap. Ludwig, myself, and six others, of whom four were tool and die makers, had to go to *Hall Schitz*.

The name of the truck factory was *Kapa-Sis,* and our work day was eight hours long.

Of course, we had much to talk about concerning these new developments. Otto informed me that he would start working tomorrow morning, and Heini Kuhnert joined us, sitting down on the grass. He was to begin his first night shift that evening.

"Well, as you can see, friends, the situation is getting serious."

"What do you expect from a worker's paradise?" Ludwig asked, sarcastically. Mouse came around the barracks, and seeing us, asked,

"Does anyone know where I can buy a shovel?" He sat down; his face deadpan.

"Are you with the shovelling brigade?" I asked.

He nodded, "Of course, did you think I wanted to dig my own grave?"

Ludwig told him about our situation, and said,

"Don't worry, Mouse, you won't be the only one who'll et blistered hands tomorrow."

"In passing, I'm supposed to send you all greetings," Mouse said. "I just visited Wihelm, and I must say, his illness really looks bad."

Otto rolled himself a cigarette, and Ludwig pulled his tobacco out too. Now came the moment Ludwig had been awaiting all day. Carefully, he tried to give Otto a demonstration of how his new *katusha* worked. On the third attempt, he lit the wick, and gave a light to the dumbfounded Otto, who couldn't remove his eyes from the *katusha*. Finally his curiosity could stand it no longer, and he asked,

"Where did you get that monstrosity?"

Ludwig let him guess for a while, then he explained.

Suddenly Ludwig's hand ran to the back of his neck, and from between his thumb and forefinger, drew out a louse. He regarded the pest for a moment, then said,

"You're still too young to die. Quick, — return to mother!"

He stuck the little pest back into his collar.

Ludwig explained to us,

"I've always been a member of the Society for the Protection of Animals."

"Otto's lucky," I said to Ludwig, "Lice don't bother him."

"Why not?" Ludwig asked, falling for the joke.

"They can't stand his stinking feet."

"You two are born comedians!" Otto said, giving us a poisonous look and acting hurt.

That night, the *powerka* was a masterpiece of military precision. Spiess Wiegand stood before us like a general on the battlefield while the brigadiers counted their brigades, reporting the full count to the barracks sergeants. They in turn marched over to Wiegand and reported. The hospital, kitchen, and other personnel were counted by the Spiess himself before the *powerka*. When Wiegand had received all reports, his mighty voice shouted,

"Later stillgestanden! Die Augen links!" (Prisoners attention! Left face!)

A final appraising look, then he reported to Major Bogoslaw. Next Bogoslaw gave the orders to his officer to check. We stood like trees at attention, without so much as a whimper. They counted us three times, and three times it was correct. The Spiess received his *"Choroscho"*, and we were left in peace.

Barracks 8 went for their soup around 6:00 the next morning, and at 7:00, we stood on the camp street staring at the prison gate while the brigadiers collected their men for the day's work. There was a sense of excitement at our first working day.

Finally, everything was ready; the gates opened while Russian soldiers waited outside the camp to take over. They placed themselves on both sides, and we started moving. We marched past the Russian garrison towards the smoking chimneys of the *Kapa-Sis*.

After a good half hour, we stood in front of an enormous gate while the plant police, armed with rifles, stopped our column. There was arguing, cursing and finally we marched through the gate. The column was stopped again in the smelting plant area while the Russian authorities bickered over us. We felt like livestock. Each supervisor demanded a certain number of workers, all claiming they were short of help. They swore, and waved their arms, finally deciding where we belonged. The prisoners for the smelting plant left, while we, who were in *Hall Schitz* were the last to leave. Determinedly, we followed our leader, marching over half completed excavations, between old tool shacks and rusting machine parts. Ludwig panted,

"I've lost my "rehabilitation" spirit even before I've begun working!"

"Finally we reached our destination and our leader spoke to a well-dressed Russian whom I later found out was the *Natschalnik* (boss) of Schitz. Unfortunately, he could not speak German, and none of us spoke enough Russian to be able to communicate with him. Helplessly, he shook his head, and then tried English.

"Does anyone speak English?"

No answer. *"Dawai!"*, he mentioned with his hand for us to follow him. We stood around for fifteen minutes while many workers stopped to stare at us.

What an enormous work hall, I thought! The hall was in a large passageway and high above hung a five ton crane. To the left and right stood the drilling and punch machines, and lathes and die machines. We were apparently the subject of much interest to the workers. They stood with their heads together, finding us highly interesting.

The *Natschalnik* reappeared with two men of markedly different characters. One was tall and strong, while the other one looked like a midget. The little one spoke to us in quite good German,

"The *Natschalnik,*" and he pointed to the neatly dressed man, "would like to know which of you are tool and die makers."

Four comrades stepped forward.

"Good," the little man said, "Follow the *Natschalnik* to his office."

Pointing to the tall man, he said, "This is Alexei, your foreman. He will show you what to do. *Gut, ja?*"

We nodded our heads enthusiastically.

Our foreman rolled himself a cigarette, and Ludwig took out his *Katusha* and gave him a light.

"Spaziba." Alexei pointed to Ludwig's lighter, saying, *"Katusha da."*

I observed our foreman whose face was covered with pock marks, looking as if a round of buckshot was imbedded in it. Our interpreter now excused himself going in to the *Natschalnik's* office.

Alexei gave us our working tools. Ludwig and I were

given a hand barrow, which is called a *Nassilki*. Our duties involved loading up the dirt, waste and scrap iron from the machinery and carrying it outside. The other two had to sweep the floors. After Alexei had learned our names, we began working immediately. Every time we carried a load outside we took a few drags on a butt and rested a few minutes. Naturally, our motions were closely watched, I could feel eyes peering down on our necks. We were anxious to make a good impression and tried to show interest in our work. The other prisoners worked conscientiously, too.

Alexei came by several times, appearing pleased with our work. In no time at all, it was noon. The sirens screamed and the workers ran to the canteen which was centrally placed and easy to reach from everywhere on the premises. While the workers ate, we prisoners sat on the grass, sucking our thumbs. My stomachs were in knots. We could not leave the hall, being forbidden to wander around.

I had some luck in the afternoon when one of the workers gave me a piece of bread and some *Machorka*. Ludwig and I sat on the scrap pile, sharing the bread. It was not very much, but I doubt if a piece of cake had ever tasted better. The afternoon passed slowly, while the beginnings of callouses began to show on my hands. Several Russians tried to talk to me, and I began to understand them. Phrasing answers was difficult, and what I couldn't say, I had to make up with gestures. All in all, I felt that we were not hated for ourselves personally. Foreman Alexei came to see us often, but since we always bummed a cigarette, he did not visit us as much as before.

Ludwig nick-named him "The Spitter" because almost each time he spoke, he cursed, then spat. But he was no ordinary spitter, like many other Russians; not by a long shot.

Alexei was an artist who spat a thin fine stream of

saliva through his teeth, always hitting his target. Ludwig was so struck by Alexei's skill, he tried to imitate him, but after two hours he had no saliva left, and gave up.

Finally, our first working day was over. The siren sounded and we were replaced by the second shift. The smelting plant workers were as black as chimney sweeps, while the rest of us were just dirty. The soldiers counted us repeatdly until they were convinced they had the right number.

Before the factory gate we were stopped while the plant police searched us. Our soldiers wanted to go home right away and started quarrelling. But the plant police won, and we were searched thoroughly before we left the premises.

Thank God, no big fuss was made once we returned to the camp. We hurried over to the barracks where the midday soup waited for us, stored in wooden barrels. We had hardly finished when it was time for "Evening soup". After gorging myself, I felt much better.

Later we were visited by Otto, Mouse and Heini. After awhile Peter showed up; his working hours were longer than ours. He said that he liked his job and told us a new transport of German prisoners was to arrive the next day. Since we were all exausted, we went to bed early. Despite the hard cot, I slept like a log. Even so, 43 lice and one flea went to their deaths before I fell asleep.

A transport of German prisoners arrived the next day and our camp now consisted of 1483 men and 123 officers. The highest ranking officer was a Berlin Luftwaffen Major by the name of Wolfshausen. The officers stayed in Barracks 20 and formed an elite class. They ate officers' rations and did not work, temporarily, anyway. Since these men wore fairly decent uniforms and wore their insignia, they continued to uphold traditional modes of conduct. It was enlightening to hear the Herr Lieutenant talk with the Herr Hauptmann. The respectable bow of the head was in order, and the quiet clicking of heels, too. The comedy reached its high point one day, when I heard two officers carrying on an impossible conversation in the latrine. Listening to them, I found myself unable to carry on my business, and hurriedly left the latrine with a belly ache. Only Major Wolfshausen impressed me sympathetically. Despite his rank he was more practical than all the other officers.

One day we returned home from work to find a great commotion in the camp. The Novotnik had called the officers for a medical examination, but they refused to be touched by a woman doctor. In return, she showed them the power of a doctor in Russia; she ordered all their heads shaved.

Naturally enough, the officers were not going to put up with this and raised a strong protest. Major Wolfshausen personally handed the complaint to the Russian command, whose answer went like this:

"The Russian command is in no way bound to any agreements, and are free to do what they think best."

After much argument among themselves, wisdom prevailed, and the officers went to the barbers. For us, it was a cause for real satisfaction to see them walking arount with bald heads. But for them it was a day of great shame. A few days later, however, the real bomb fell. All of the officers, except Major Wolfshausen, were assigned to work. Several were made brigadiers, while others were given technical positions, such as engineers, architects, etc., according to their education. There was a captain in the camp who was an artist; he was permitted to paint. His pictures were sold in the city and his share of the money kept his tobacco pouch full. An elderly Lieutenant who had been a school teacher by profession, taught speech and diction. Lieutenant Manfred von Bulow was his name, and he spoke six languages, including Russian. Lieutenant von Bulow was assigned to the administration building and worked closely with Peter. As fate would have it, von Bulow was destined to play a part in the biggest scandal in the history of Camp 6/10.

Our camp was officially designated as self-supporting. This meant that every able-bodied prisoner was paid according to his work. Of course, we did not receive any cash for our work, but in order to eat a full ration every day, the prisoner had to fulfill his norm. The so-called *nariat* was a written statement indicating what percentage of the norm the prisoner had fulfilled, and was signed by an authorized person in the factory.

Working conditions were generally poor in Russia and the norm system unrealistic. Tools were often primitive and men were substituted for machines. The methods of production were characterized by a great deal of waste and inefficiency.

Twice, the smelting plant's entire monthly quota was scrapped because of a miscalculation by someone higher up. I had heard such unbelievable stories before from our construction brigades. Poor organization, incompetence, and indifference were the main reasons for a low production rate, accompained by high expenditures and waste.

Driven by the monthly production figures, the community housing project was forced to carry on through the bitterly cold Siberian winter. Bricklaying in temperatures of 23 below zero was a ridiculous undertaking. The storage and handling of building materials was a crime; there was a complete lack of order and foresight. Materials were exposed to the weather and were ruined by the time they were needed.

Then in the spring, money and time had to be spent repairing the wasteful results.

I have mentioned the difficulties some brigades had in trying to achieve 100% norm. In many cases, it was entirely up to the cleverness of the brigadier to squeeze a good *nariat* out of the boss. For instance: The Black Brigades at

Kapa-Sis had no trouble in averaging a 120% *nariat* over a year's period. While the snow shovelling brigades hardly ever reached a meager 80%. Snow shovelling in Russia is as hopeless as emptying Lake Erie with a bucket.

Peter, Otto and Heini were among those who escaped the squeeze of the *nariat* system. They were not hungry, while Ludwig, Mouse and myself were poor as church mice.

I asked Peter about Lieutenant von Bulow.

"He's quite an intelligent man", Peter said, "He speaks Russian so beautifully, it lingers in your ears."

"We don't have to worry about our officers." Otto said, "Hair or no hair, they'll figure out someway to get along."

Ludwig did not agree.

"I think the Russians are going to give them a hard time."

"Perhaps, but don't forget, losing hair doesn't mean they can't think any more!"

In the course of the years as a prisoner of war, I experienced much and accepted much that I would have considered unbelievable before my imprisonment. Russia is a vast and mysterious country and the Russian way of life often appears very strange and unreasonable to a German.

The average Russian, and I mean the people I worked with, was constantly in need of the basic necessities of life. Consequently, anything which was not nailed and tied down, disappeared quicker than a pigeon can fly. Of course, the governement viewed things differently. I learned of a Russian laborer who was given a two-year sentence because he stole five pounds of flour. Stealing potatoes from a field is considered so serious, the crime is severely punished.

In 1947, there occurred an incident in the camp which was remembered long afterwards. A brigade of German prisoners had the opportunity to exchange their wooden clod-hoppers for some leather shoes which had been discovered in an open boxcar. No one was in sight, and the exchange was quickly made. Unfortunately, the prisoners were seen and apprehended by the plant police who arrested them. Our camp command was powerless to help the brigade, and the case was taken to court. The brigadier was given ten years in prison; all the others received six years and we never saw these men again. At that time, 1947, a pair of good work shoes cost a small fortune.

The idea of "stealing" is foreign to the Russian mind. It was all explained to me very well by a Russian factory worker who said that everyone knew in Russia there was no private ownership. Everything belongs to the state, and the people are the state! The problem is, he continued, the goods are still not quite properly divided. Therefore, it was an obligation for everyone to do his part to correct the balance!

"Quite so," said his neighbor, "You have to be careful, even shaking hands with people. Make sure to count your fingers afterwards." He laughed and walked away.

It also reminded me of the way we did things in the army. We never used the word "stealing"; we called it "organization", "replacement", "relocation", or even "borrowing", but never stealing!

The morale in Camp 6/10 became worse from day to day, and three Sundays after starting to work at *Kapa-Sis,* we did not know what a day of rest was. The Black Brigade, in particular, was driven without let-up. From Monday to Saturday, we worked in *Kapa-Sis,* like mules; then on Sunday, we were loaded into trucks and sent to work on the collective farms.

There we received soup around noon time, and went back to work for the rest of the day. In the field, we ate as much as our stomachs could hold; cabbages, turnips and carrots.

Modern farm machinery was not available; we were cheaper to use. What I did not know then, was that this Sunday labor did not have the approval of the Soviet government. Our Russian camp commander did this on his own initiative.

It was only natural that the sick list and mortality rate rose rapidly. The word "escape" could be heard more and more frequently, and plans were laid and calculations discussed. It was the general opinion that our chances of escape were poor. But for awhile, this hope helped us to bear the ordeal of prison life. The idea caught like wildfire, and went like fever through the camp.

Apparently we had underestimated the Russian command. Nor did we consider the sizable number of spies and informers among us.

One night, while the roll-call was being taken, the Russian command conducted a surprise search in the barracks.

It looked as if the entire garrison had been called in to do the job. During the investigation, we were ordered to stand in our places. No incriminating evidence was found but two prisoners were interrogated. Blows were applied, but no information was gained from them. One prisoner lay for weeks afterwards in the hospital with a broken nose and cracked ribs. The Russians usually turned up knives, lightbulbs, straight razors, pieces of sawblades, and various instruments "borrowed" from the factory; none of which they actually sought. All of these items were worth a great deal to us however. The Russians took everything, and punishments were handed out freely; brigades were broken up and jobs reassigned.

For several days, the whole camp was in an uproar. All plans for escape had to be postponed indefinitely. Instead we applied our energies to ferreting out the spies and informers. We managed to turn up a few; but wisely, did not expose them. We knew the G.P.U. would just replace them with new ones, and it was wiser to keep the ones we already had, knowing who they were.

A new development: Barracks 2 was fenced off. Soon we discovered why — we were being presented with a brig. A prison within a prison. A high fence with an abundance of barbed wire was erected around Barracks 2, and the entrance was a heavy door with a big lock. Soon the first prisoners were led into this jail. For unknown reasons, they were jailed for five days and put on rations of 200 grams of bread a day, and soup only twice a day.

We had our own laws within the barracks, and stealing bread was the lowest thing one prisoner could do to another. If the thief was caught, he could be sure of being beaten up — then he was treated as a pariah.

After the surprise raid, the camp seethed with discontent. The Russians must have felt that now was the time to give us a little rope, and promptly. Therefore, the following Sunday was our first day of rest.

Spiess Wiegand was called to the G.P.U.; they considered him responsible for the low morale in the camp. Chief Purga offered him the choice of doing something about it, or going to work with the Black Brigade. At any rate, the Spiess was supposed to form a culture group. Singing, so the G.P.U. thought, was *Choroscho Cultura.*

That Sunday night after the *powerka,* the Spiess, introduced his plan, requesting everyone with theatrical or musical backgrounds to report to Barracks 6.

Ludwig and I discussed whether we should go. He was astonished when I said I was interested, and even more so, when I mentioned I had occasionally performed on the stage.

"As what?" he asked mockingly, "Pulling curtains?"

"Something like that." I replied. "Really, my brief career in the theater began in Norway. It started one day when I sat around with my buddies, on kitchen duty, peeling potatoes. To compensate for this boring task, we tried to amuse each other by telling jokes, singing, and so forth. Apparently, the corporal on duty overheard us, and before I knew it, I was on the stage rehearsing for the Christmas Show."

"How did it come out?" asked Ludwig, the limelight seeker.

"The soldiers' paper in Norway gave us an excellent review."

"And after that?"

"Later I acted in skits and also played comedy roles."

Ludwig said, "Well, Buster Keaton, let's get over there then!"

Spiess Wiegand's voice drowned the barracks chatter,

"Men," he began, "The purpose of this meeting is to lay the ground work for a culture group. I personally am devoted to the German lieder. If anyone here has been a conductor or musician, will he please report to me. Those interested in the chorus please step to the left; in the theatre group, to the right."

A heated discussion began among the heavily represented patrons of the arts. Five men reported to Spiess Wiegand. Of these, two were chosen. The first was introduced to us as August Rohdenbach. He was a stage architect with excellent references. The other Willi Brandenburg, was to be the leader of the men's chorus, he had been a singing teacher and chorus director before the war.

Ludwig and I were undecided about which group to join. More out of curiosity than artistic inclination, we decided to cast our lot with Rohdenbach. The lieutenant pulled out a pencil and notebook, luxury articles in the camp, and jotted down our names. Next to each name he listed the particular talent of the individual. Ludwig was a reciter, while I was given a "Z.B.V.," which roughly translated meant, "utility man".

Rohdenbach already had a rough idea of what he would like to do, but first a great deal of support was necessary from the Russian command. In some miraculous way, we would have to build a stage. When things got going, he would notify us; then we were dismissed.

The next Sunday was beautiful and clear and we didn't have to work. The men's chorus spent the day rehearsing behind Barracks 6. Brandenburg tried to fashion a chorus of tolerable voices, and the friends of song practiced long and hard; after the *powerka*, the chorus entertained with two German folksongs.

The first one was rather good, but the second needed more practice. Despite this, the prison audience applauded heartily.

Otto said thoughtfully, "They do quite well for a first attempt. Don't you think so?"

Ludwig answered, "Yes, they sing like canaries."

The real surprise was Wiegand whose tenor voice was by far the most powerful and clearest. I noticed that Peter was especially cheerful. When I asked him the reasons for his happiness, he answered,

"I'm happy because Krauskopf isn't singing with them!"

All in all, I felt it was a good day; the best we had known since arriving in Tscheljabinsk.

Because of the rearrangement of the brigades, Ludwig and I spent a week working at odd jobs around Tscheljabinsk. On one occasion, we were told to unload a boxcar of nails. After we had opened the door, which was quite an undertaking, we were astonished to find that the nails were unpacked. We stared helplessly at a mountain of metal spikes. Now I could understand how a hungry fox feels when it faces a bristling hedgehod. The Russian foreman scratched his head, spat a few times, and muttered a helpless *"Job twoju matj."*

After procuring some crosspicks, two wheelbarrows, and shovels, the foreman suddenly remembered a lot of paperwork. With a *"Dawai Kamerad!"*, he excused himself, cursed the nails again, and hurried off.

For a time, we made no progress at all.

Ludwig suggested, "What we need is a stick of dynamite!"

After we had attacked the pile from all angles, we were finally able to push a metal plate onto the floor of the box car; from then on our progress was more satisfactory. We stabbed at the pile like mad men, dragging the nails onto the plate and from there the shovelling was easy.

Soon the foreman came around again to check our work. He was overjoyed by the progress we were making and gave us all some tobacco, promising to write a good *nariat* if we emptied the car in good time. There was an arrangement worked out with the camp whereby he could detain us until the work was finished. Also, the firm had to feed us. At noon, we were led to the Stalowa where we received *kascha*, soup and bread.

By 6:00 p.m. we finished unloading; it had been a long shift. Half dead from exhaustion, we crept back to camp.

Another day we had to unload cement. Of course, they wanted us to perform a miracle here also. The cement was loose and the wind blew it about in all directions, including our eyes and mouth. We tasted cement for three days afterwards. One should be a POW in Russia to experience the marvellous taste of cement, combined with fish soup!

That evening, Peter brought us the good news that Ludwig and I would be returning to *Schitz*. He said *Schitz* was willing to pay more for us. Also, the work force would be enlarged. We were quite happy about this.

Ludwig said, "After all those terrible jobs, I'll be glad to see Alexei, the Spitter, again!"

Our brigade now consisted of ten men, and it was wonderful to see how we were greeted when we entered the *Schitz-Hall*. Alexei gave us some tobacco, saying with a broad smile,

"*Job twoju matj!* Where the hell have you two been!"

Almost everyone in the factory had a friendly word for us, including the women.

Luba Czernikow, a machine operator, asked me where I had been, and I tried to answer her with my limited Russian vocabulary. With the help of some fancy pantomime, I think she understood.

Ludwig and I made ourselves more *Katushas* from materials "organized" within the factory. I gave one to Otto who accepted it happily. In the course of the next month, Ludwig and I made quite a few more and sold each of them for six hundred grams of bread. It was a good deal, and a welcome addition to our meagre fare.

Once it rained for three days without stopping and the main street of the camp was a river of mud. Nothing but muck and water as far as the eye could see. I was one of the few in camp who received a pair of rubber galoshes. Under normal weather conditions they would have been very useful, but when the ground was muddy, they were treacherous, and I sailed along on them like Charlie Chaplin, in one of his old movies.

As always in life, even this misery passed and the rain stopped. The sun quickly dried up the swamp that our surroundings had become. The camp life began to develop a more obvious character — extremes of squalor and comfort took on definable features. While daily men died of hunger and sickness, the upper classes in the camp fared increasingly well.

In our camp was a German dentist named Dr. Bratsch. He conducted his profession in the camp. The Russians found him a dilapidated drilling machine which had to be worked by treadle. The Russian officers had their dental care free and in return looked aside while Dr. Bratsch practiced on his own. He was a competent dentist indeed; to get an appointment depended mainly upon one's position, or the amount of rubles in one's pocket.

One day when I visited Otto, I observed a gold cap on one of his front teeth. From him I found out that quite a few POW's had managed to keep their wedding rings, which they eventually sold. The poor soul who parted sorrowfully with his wedding ring received for it two month's double rations of soup and kascha, and an increased bread ration based on the quality of the gold. These rings came into Dr. Bratsch's possession through mysterious channels and were melted down for crowns on the teeth of the higher-ups.

What could a hungry man do? Tortured by conscience and hounded by the longing for a crust of bread, a man would even steal from corpses. I remember one incident very clearly when a prisoner lay on his bunk talking to a neighbor, and suddenly died of a heart attack. His friend did not report the death immediately, but waited until after meal time when he collected the rations of the dead man as well as his own. Only after he had eaten his fill did he report the death to the barracks sergeant.

From Wilhelm, I learned what hunger could do to men in the hospital. Once while I sat on his bed, talking to him, he leaned over and said.

"Kurt, you won't believe this, but there are characters here who are real mental cases over food. They play games about it and dream constantly of elaborate feasts. It's incredible."

I was interested, but still did not fully understand.

"What do you mean?"

"These jokers spend most of the day sleeping, but in the evening they take out the food which they have stored all day, and gather around the table, as though for a banquet. They go to ridiculous extremes, even issuing formal invitations by way of mouth for this fiesta.

"After polite formalities, the dinner party begins. Each of them brings a piece of plywood (which is used as a plate) to the table. Paper thin slices of bread are arranged around their improvised plates; each slice is a show piece in itself! Here is a morsel of soup, there, a touch of kascha. Some slices of toast are carefully burnt so that a pattern manifests itself. Occasionally, someone may have a green onion or turnip which he cuts up and uses to adorn his entry. No one has eaten so much as a nibble yet. Now you have an idea of what occurs!"

"What happens next?" I asked, with curiosity.

"The real test of nerves begins. No one actually eats; they just take an occasionnal nibble from their slices. Apparently, the last to finish is the champion. Most of the time is spent talking about food. They paint pictures of sumptuous feasts, rare wines, exquisite cakes and delicacies. Recently two officers joined the club who knew quite a bit about foreign cooking. You can't imagine how the others almost fainted with sheer delight while officers threw about French words describing delicious gourmet dishes. And ironically all they have before them is kascha, soup and bread! The quickest way to get yourself thrown out of the club, though, is to joke about women. Well, Kurt, doesn't that make you nauseous?"

"Yes, Wilhelm it's no wonder you're still sick!"

Wilhelm face became serious. Softly, he said,

"Kurt, I'll never be well again."

"Nonsense, Wilhelm!" I said. "Don't talk like that!"

Wilhelm waved his hand resignedly.

"I've got bleeding ulcers, Kurt, and there's no cure here in Siberia." Then he said, "Keep it to yourself, Kurt. Promise?"

I woved to say nothing. When I left him I returned with a heavy heart to the barracks.

August Rohdenbach became our culture group director and soon showed himself to be an extraordinary, ambitious man. He was also in charge of a brigade of carpenters and cabinet makers who worked in Tscheljabinsk, and made beautiful furniture. They exceeded their norms and even earned rubles as extra commissions. Later Rohdenbach and his brigade were given an entire barracks which was turned into a carpenter shop. The machinery was "organized" from the outside while the camp leadership looked away, sometimes even lending a helping hand. They always had more than they could handle and business prospered while Rohdenbach became a camp celebrity. Along with Wiegand and the doctors, he had a room all to himself.

It was not long before our first variety show was performed on a Sunday evening. The stage was simple and so was the production. Rohdenbach was the witty master of ceremonies and played his part well. Ludwig did two of his recitations and was well received. The chorus sang two songs and an Austrian imitated a famous comedian and was roundly applauded. I did a parody of a woman undressing in front of a mirror; the audience liked that too. Next five pyramid acrobats performed; their act was well done, but the bodies of the performers were not too convincing. We finished the evening by singing along with the chorus, the German song: *"Drum Brüder eine gute Nacht."* We had the feeling that we were headed in the right direction. The prisoners were grateful; their applause was our reward.

Judging by all signs, Camp 6/10 was used as a transit camp. Prisoners were always coming and going and it was a great surprise to us when Major Wolfshausen, the highest ranking officer in the camp, was transferred. The rumor circulated that he had been sent to a camp for staff officers.

One of the late comers was named Paul Finke. He and another man called Erich Wetzlaff laid the foundations for the antifacistic organization in the camp. Both of them claimed to have been long standing members of the Communist Party. They also bragged of their experiences in a German concentration camp. The Russian command gave these two men their full support.

Ludwig and I advanced in a small way too; Alexei, the Spitter, took us off sweeping ,and put us in production. I operated a big drilling machine while Ludwig was taught to use the sheet metal cutters. Our principal work, however, was to keep Schitz supplied with raw materials. As soon as the iron came from the smelting plant it had to be softened, marked, then delivered to the machine operators. The work was interesting and the time passed quickly.

One day we received a helper; a young Russian by the name of Kostja. He was about nineteen. Unfortunately, he was not too industrious but he compensated for it by his strong belief in Ludwig and me. In fact, he trusted us so much that whenever the work piled up, he left quickly. Sometimes he walked away with a piece of iron he was supposed to deliver and never returned that day. Once, shortly before quitting time, he returned to find Alexei still with us. Quickly Kostja took his handkerchief from his pocket and wiped his dry face.

"Boy!" he exclaimed, "What a day I had!"

Weakly, as if overcome with exhaustion, he asked Alexei for a cigarette.

Once I had to take Kostja with me to the smelting plant to pick up the iron for Schitz. We arrived there around nine o'clock. After the iron was loaded into a large metal box we chalk marked it. "Schitz". Next we had to find the crane leader to lift it onto the truck waiting to transport it to the plant.

The crane leader was a heavy-set, powerfully built man, and by all signs, a very busy one. I sent Kostja over, and the crane leader barked at him,

"You'll just have to wait! I have to look after my own people first, just relax!"

This was the line Kostja had been waiting for, and soon found himself a cozy spot behind the furnace and settled down to sleep. He commanded,

"Wake me up when he's ready!"

Then he curled up like a cat, and was lost to the world.

I stood at my station like a soldier on the banks of the Volga, not daring to move lest I miss the crane leader. I now was able to observe my surroundings. Never in my life had I been in a smelting plant. What I saw was the noisiest, filthiest, and most dangerous place imaginable. All around were stamping machines, oil baths, presses, furnaces, and hydraulic hammers. It took me awhile to adjust to the noise, the light, and the suffocating smoke. Later I learned that accidents were the rule, here, not the exception.

The crane operator high above in the crane case, worked as a team with a man on the ground the man who applied the chains. They communicated by means of a fiery torch which the man below used to indicate the direction the crane was supposed to go.

Red hot iron was removed from the furnaces and cast into shapes by a gigantic, power-driven hammer. I watched a team of three. Two men tossed about heavy pieces of iron with large tongs, while the third operated the hammer. They were artists in their own way. Undoubtedly, the work was heavy, but to me it appeared merely child's play.

Through the years, many German prisoners died or were crippled here. The heroes of the "Rehabilitation Brigade" died with honor in the Worker's Paradise.

Around noon our foreman, Alexei, showed up and I had just enough time to awaken Kostja. Alexei was anxious because the iron from the smelting plant had not arrived, and asked Kostja for an explanation. Kostja acted as if he were exhausted, and said, disappointedly.

"We followed the crane leader all around, begging him. We practically got down on our knees pleading with him to take care of us, but all our efforts were in vain. Boy, I'm beat! You ask Kurt if I'm lying!"

Alexei's critical eyes fell on me and I was so astonished by the range of Kostja's imagination that I could only nod my head. Around two o'clock in the afternoon, the crane leader finally attached the chains to our box and five minutes later it was on its way to Schitz.

CHAPTER EIGHT

The warm weather came to an end abruptly. Now we had cool evenings and cold nights. The Russians warned us that winter was on its way and at the same time, the health situation in the camp was deteriorating. The Russians were contemplating building an extension to the hospital because more and more men were falling sick and the toll of dead and injured was frightening.

Peter told me confidentially that a transport of prisoners would soon be going home. A week later, Lidia Novotnik selected prisoners from the hospital for the transport and I was happy that Wilhelm was among them. When he spoke to me about it, I saw a shimmer of hope in his eyes.

Naturally, the transport home produced much excitement among us. Many were of the opinion that this was a good sign, indicating there still was some hope for the rest of us. Some prisoners became reckless and concluded that from now on the sick would be sent home as a matter of course. Therefore, they subjected their already weakened systems to ordeals that would completely break down their health. They exchanged their bread rations for tobacco and salt knowing that eliminating the bread was the quickest way to becoming ill.

The Russians soon found out about this and there was a surprise raid in which all the salt was confiscated. They also carted off everything else they came across — as usual. Punishments were freely meted out and some prisoners were interrogated.

Many of the unfortunate prisoners who had indulged themselves, now had to pay a high price for this folly. No more transports were sent home in 1945, and these prisoners found themselves defenseless against the cruel winter. Many died because of this scheme.

The first snow came earlier than expected; it was only a warning of worse hardships to come. There were a few more fair days; then the east wind informed us that winter was coming fast. Winter clothes were issued in a hurry.

Gloves, padded jackets, padded trousers, felt boots, furlined caps, and a fur coat, comprised our entire winter wardrobe. On the left arm of the lined jacket and coat were the russian initials for P.O.W. The fur coat was a blessing. Though inconvenient to work in, it was excellent against the wind and cold. And at night it was a marvellous blanket.

The boots were made out of a single piece of felt with no heels or extra sole. Very simple and practical, but only for cold weather.

Firewood was another serious problem because the camp command provided us with very little fuel. We had to look after ourselves. Day after day, an endless stream of trains rolled by, laden with coal from the mines; but we saw very little of it in our barracks. The work brigades pilfered firewood whenever they found it.

The brigade most desperately in need of firewood was the wash brigade. The wash house was located outside the camp palisade, near the local army garrison. I learned about their condition through a friend who worked there. Each worker had a washtub, board, and a single piece of soap about the size of a half a pound of butter. Each man had to fulfill his norm to get his 600 gram ration of bread. In the summer the work was not too bad, but in winter it was virtually impossible to earn more than four hundred grams of bread a day. The big problem was hot water because there was no wood and very little coal to make a fire. Wood pilfering was essential for this brigade to carry on its work.

Once they sawed down two poles intended for high power lines, and chopped them immediately into firewood. The city raised a ruckus, and accused the wash brigade. Surprisingly, the camp leadership protected the wash brigade arguing the brigade could not have done such dirty work! During the day they worked under the protective eyes of the army garrison, and at night they were locked up in the camp.

My buddy was later transferred from this unremunerative work. In his next medical he was so emaciated that the Novotnik ordered him in the kitchen to get some meat on his bones. Ludwig and I however, remained in the same work class. By now, though, we knew that during working hours, there existed ways of obtaining something to eat. As I mentioned, women worked in the plant too. Ludwig and I helped them to lift heavy objects and were very courteous to them. It often paid off in food and tobacco.

Luba Czernikow was one that I especially liked. She always had a friendly smile for me and often a piece of bread too. Nor were our tobacco problems as bad as before. Alexei, the Spitter, was our source of supply. One day, he asked me what front I had served on.

"The Finland front," I answered.

"Finland front?" Alexei was surprised, and spat aimlessly on the floor. Then opening his shirt, he pointed to a long, ugly scar. 'Maybe you were the son of a bitch who gave me this!"

"I was an infantryman, not an artilleryman!" I declared. Alexei smiled, and a moment later, I showed him the wounds on my back.

"Is it possible that you caused these?" I asked.

"Of course not! I was in the infantry too!"

We laughed, smoked his tobacco, and had a mutual understanding.

The friendships with Mouse, Heini Kuhnert and Otto gradually dwindled. It was only natural since each of us had gone his own way. My only true friends were Peter and Ludwig. Peter came as often as he could to my barracks, seldom empty-handed. Information about new developments was his specialty, and from him we learned that Finke and Wetzlaff were often in conference with the G.P.U.

"Kurt, those two boot-lickers are after something. I wish I knew what it was."

We did not have long to wait; the anti-fascist organization — abbreviated Antifa — received its own barracks. Finke and Wetzlaff took up headquarters there making themselves responsible for political advertising, morale, and cultural activities. The Antifa grew in no time. Positions were liberally dispensed and hand-made badges given out freely. Finke and Wetzlaff each wore a polished brass "A" while their subordinates had to settle for nickel ones.

Quite a few prisoners saw the oportunity to gain advantages for themselves and they grabbed at positions in the new organization. Suddenly they were completely dedicated to Communism! Many of them vowed that in their hearts they had always wanted to be members of Communist Party, but had been afraid to join!

The Antifa wanted to impress the camp so Finke, Wetzlaff and Rohdenbach decided to initiate a bang-up variety show. They drew up plans for a new stage, but there was also the problem of obtaining musical instruments. At this point, Finke and Wetzlaff were able to show their genius for organization.

Finke was a propagandist and politician of high caliber who could speak without tiring and surpass everyone in conjuring up empty slogans. After the evening roll call he stood before the camp, shouting,

"Men! We are faced with a crisis of enormous magnitude. The future weeks will require sacrifices from all culture-minded comrades! As workers we must contribute every ounce of cooperation in our common enterprise. The problem is this — the great cultural work cannot move forward without a stage. We need the labor of your hands, the ingenuity of your brains, and the quintessence of your dedication. We need every light bulb, nail and every helping hand. I, personally, will give up half of my bread ration until the stage is completed!" Somehow the idea took fire, and we slaved to build that stage. Rodenbach's brigade worked every free hour around the clock. Everybody was so involved, that only a few noticed that the bread rations were now a little smaller and more moist.

The Russian command showed their approval of the project by giving us bed sheets which we converted into a stage curtain, and the Russian officer corps donated a guitar and a violin. Rohdenbach used his influence, approaching the camp big shots and collecting contributions for an accordion. One day, he accomplished the impossible, appearing with a brand new instrument. It was rumored that he had made up the additional cost by building some custom-made furniture.

About a dozen accordionists answered the call and an open competition was held. However, all the contestants paled before the true artist of the squeeze-box, Konrad Kohlmeyer, whose ability was fantastic. The presence of the accordion was invigorating, and musicians of all sorts stepped forward. We even had a former orchestra leader and music teacher who organized a band. The German intelligence and love of the Muse awoke and began to play an active part in camp life. The Austrians did not stay in the background either and we welcomed them with open arms.

Ludwig practiced two new recitation pieces while I rehearsed a clown role. I also had to do a skit as a woman. The tailors did their very best to outfit me as a woman; a horsehair wig and a pair of falsies did a lot to improve my role as a "good time girl".

Slowly, but surely, the program took shape. A reporter from a well known German magazine was also a

prisoner and with the approval of the G.P.U. he published a hand-written newspaper which was posted in the
culture house. The variety program was given a lot of
attention and plenty of advertising space. The premiere
was to be the second day in November.

The Siberian winter, with a great deal of snow and
bitter cold, made its debut. The stiff wind from the east
blew without mercy, even through our fur clothing. Sometimes I felt that I was walking around naked, I felt so
chilled. Frost bite of all descriptions appeared on our
bodies; noses and cheeks were generally the first hit.
There was an unwritten law among us that each one
watch over his neighbor and tell him the danger signs.
During one snow storm, my eyelids actually froze together.

Ludwig and I were lucky that we did not have to
work with an outside brigade. I can remember only one
occasion when the outdoor details were not sent out to
work. That was when the temperature dropped to 65
degrees below zero. Dr. Meinicke informed me that the
percentage of essential ingredients in our food were
minute; even to inhale the cold air requires energy to
warm it up; muscular atrophy reigned triumphant. In
the next de-lousing, I was shocked to see how frail
the bone structure of my comrades was; nor were
Ludwig and I spared the deterioration. In the next medical examination, we were demoted to Class 3/6. The
work brigades were reassigned new work and separated
from each other. It was a painful and very confusing
procedure. "Schitz" was now manned only by a 3/6
brigade, losing two excellent lathe workers who still belonged to Class 2. The smelter plant still used Class 2
workers only. After our shift was completed, we had to
sit around for two hours until the others in the smelting
plant had finished their day. Because of this the guards
were nervous and short-tempered, and it was, in this

period that I received the beating by the Tartar which I mentioned previously.

Finally, after several confused days, the situation was solved. The 3/6 men became civilian guards and we went home directly after our shifts were over.

At long last each barracks was assigned a small coal ration truly a gift from heaven. For a little while it was nice and cozy. Of course, the bodies of so many prisoners generated a certain amount of heat, too. The wash brigade could also breathe easier. For a while anyway, they were able to scrub up a full ration of bread.

The influential members of the camp could easily be recognized. They held the best positions, wore the best clothing and started to comb their hair again. But periodically, even these were "purged" by the sudden whim of Russian comand. After a little while, however, the comb was in evidence again.

Every camp has a certain number of skillful people who can make something out of nothing. In our camp, they made combs, mirrors, polished brass rings, folding knives and many other useful things, and the clientele they served were usually the aristocrats of the camp. The Russian guards also profited indirectly from this trade whenever they conducted a search-and-seize party. Usually they were looking for quite different things, but they liked what they saw so much they couldn't give them up.

Despite hunger, snow, and the rising death toll, the cultural developments in our camp progressed. The motivating drive came from the higher-ups, while the hungry ones were pulled along by sheer momentum.

We staged a dress rehearsal, and four days later came the premiere performance. Rohdenbach gave me a lot of support in my clown role. At first the Russians were opposed to the ending, because a big knife was stuck into my back. Naturally, there was a thick board under my clothing to protect me, but the Russians were apprehensive about it. The board was certainly large and thick enough, but none of the actors who played the role of assassin knew how to aim. Many times the knife came close enough to turn a comedy into a tragedy.

The dress rehearsal showed up many defects in the production but Rohdenbach assured us that this is usually the case. He was right; the premiere performance went off like a time bomb.

The Russian authorities attended the performance, also the German camp aristocracy, followed by those who had donated their free hours to make the production a reality.

The unanimous opinion was that our performance was a tremendous success and the Russians praised it, while the camp newspaper gave us an excellent review.

A miracle happened; over night I became a celebrity! It took me a while to grasp the reversal of my situation and finally I realized I was not dreaming. People began treating me with more respect; I was even given some new names. Before the program began, I had been announced as "Knüppel" the clown — that name never left me. My role as a good time girl was not overlooked either, and I also received a nick-name for that. From that night on, the Russians called me "Jena" (Woman). All the doors were finally opening to me, and I received my first treat from Spiess Wiegand. That same night, I was able to sleep without feeling pangs of hunger.

One night, Finke and Wezlaff invited me to their quarters. To my surprise, I found myself conversing with them over tea and toast liberally covered with a thick layer of sugar. I also smoked freely the tobacco placed on the table for our use. I no longer had to wait in line at the barber's. When I showed up, I was immediately given the next free chair.

"After all," the barber said, "Ladies first!"

One day Heini Kuhnert said to me, "Knüppel, if you ever feel hungry, don't forget I'm still working in the kitchen."

After one of the performances, Rohdenback invited

me to play chess with him. While we were playing, I commented on the chess pieces.

"They are nice, aren't they, Knüppel. I'll let you in on a little secret. I'm going to have these same pieces duplicated in 60 centimeter sizes, next summer we're going to play chess in the open. A large chess board built outdoors and the pieces will be moved about by large, two-pronged forks with long handles. What do you think of that?"

"I think it's a fantastic idea!"

"Knüppel," he went on, "We're just at the beginning. I have great plans. I'm going to create a theatre group they'll talk about for years to come, that I promise you!" He paused, then said, "Since we're on the subject of the theater, may I congratulate you on your performance. It's a pleasure watching you."

"Thanks, August. But don't forget, I couldn't have done it without your help."

"Think nothing of it, Knüppel. You've got a natural talent but it definitely should be developed, especially your movements and timing."

"Yes. I suppose so."

Finally, we got down to chess, and I discovered shortly that August was by far the superior player. When I lost my third game, I gave up. Before parting, though, Rohdenbach gave me 600 grams of bread to take along.

Ludwig was still awake, and while we shared the bread, I told him about August's plans. He listened, and agreed that I had boarded the right ship.

"Looks that way, doesn't it?" I said, "And its clear sailing too."

Before I fell asleep, I thought over what my friends had said to me on opening night. How had Peter put it?

"Kurt, you were simply magnificent! I'm proud to

Otto's approach was more blunt. He slapped me so be your friend."

hard on the shoulder, my falsies nearly jumped out of my dress.

"Hi there, Lilli Marlene! Could I ask you out for dinner sometime?"

Then he winked at me.

The Mouse from Dresden confessed that I reminded him of a girl he used to go with.

This thought alone was quite amusing, and with a smile on my lips, I turned over on my sleeping side.

But sleep did not come, so many things had happened to me these last few days! I needed time to sort things out and put them in their proper places; I was caught in a whirlpool of doubts, while my conscience was persistently demanding recognition.

My place was with the have-nots, and "genuine assholes," as Kindermann would have put it. Deep in my heart I despised the high and mighty who were our leaders. I detested their shrewdness and unscrupulous treatment of the "little" man.

I tortured myself with guilt because I had sat at their table, played chess with them, and had eaten their sugar. Finally I climbed from my bed and sat before the crackling stove. After I had lit a cigarette, I began to remember a newspaper story I had read many years before. A father and son, both roofers, had been working together on a church tower. Somehow the son lost his balance and hung on to his father for dear life. Finally, the father's strength gave out, and it was impossible to hold onto his son anymore. Now, in danger of losing his own life, the father kicked away his own flesh and blood. His son fell to his death, and the father was then able to save himself. My struggle for survival had now become a moral issue.

The days flew by, and the Russian winter gripped our hearts. Many serious frostbite cases were sent to the hospital. The newest horror was a frightening outbreak of tuberculosis which went through the camp like a forest fire. The Russians were helpless to stop the increasing number of cases. Dr. Meinicke's plea for X-ray equipment was either not heard by the Novotnik, or ignored by the authorities. The camp newspaper, *Der Lagerspiegel* (The Camp Mirror) published an article about this which was immediately suppressed by the G.P.U. The author had to report to them and was practically cut to ribbons. He was accused of trying to spread panic and words like "demoralization", "sabotage" and "inciting to revolt" were thrown at him. He was given ten days in the brig but later he was allowed to publish the paper again. From then on, the G.P.U. examined each written word with a magnifying glass.

The last performance of our program was given and I felt we outdid ourselves. The entire cast gathered afterwards and had some fun. Practically all of us still wore our costumes and for a while we lived in a different world. There was singing and dancing to music. As a woman I was the center of attraction and accepted dances continually. I played my role to the hilt and we had a lot of fun.

Ludwig invited me to dance; he was very proper and courteous. We danced to the tango, "Jealousy," and after some steps, it was clear that Ludwig really was an excellent dancer. We understood each other right away, and performed a fantasy tango that amazed everyone, ourselves included. I had never before had the desire nor the opportunity to dance as a woman. Evidently, I had buried myself completely in my role, taking it seriously. Rohdenbach suggested to me at a rehearsal,

"Knüppel, you can play the part of a Napoleon only when you fully believe that you are Napoleon!"

His words remained with me and were a tremendous help when I played other roles.

After the dance, Rohdenbach joined us, and out of nowhere asked,

"How would you two like to rehearse this number for the next program?"

We stared at him, and carried away by his own ideas, he told us what he had in mind,

"Ludwig, you, of course, will have to wear long tails; and you, Knüppel, must wear a white evening gown."

His thoughts moved about in an atmosphere entirely unfamiliar to us. He glowed with ideas, drawing us a picture that would have made Cecil B. DeMille look like an amateur.

Regretfully, the evening was over and we parted happily, looking forward to another successful program. For several hours we had forgotten the dreariness of our situation. I had a personal reason to be grateful, as this day, November 30th, was my twenty-fifth birthday.

Early in December arrangements were under way for a Christmas program. It was decided that we would present a short Christmas program which would be of a religious nature. As fate would have it, I was unable to take part in this joyous occasion. It came about this way:

It started out to be an ordinary working day at Schitz — like many others. Kostja, Ludwig and I brought the iron from the smelting plant to Schitz, working with a 2-ton crane. Kostja was on the switch-box of the crane, while I fastened the chains to the box holding the iron. Kostja must have inadvertently pressed the button which lifted the crane before I was ready. Suddenly, the heavy box tilted towards me, and instinctively, I put my hands before me for protection. A heavy piece of iron fell over, entrapping my left hand in the box. An incredible pain raced through my entire body and blood gushed all over the iron. Ludwig cried out in German, *"Halt! Halt!"*

When my injured hand was freed, I bent over like a jackknife, holding it with my other hand. That's as much as I can remember. People recovering from their initial shock, snapped into action. Ludwig helped me to sit down, while someone put a cigarette between my lips. Luba Czernikow wrapped a scarf around my hand, and bent my arm into an upright position to slow down the bleeding. Supported by Ludwig and Alexei, who had hurried over, I was led to the First Aid Station.

The First Aid Station was located near the smelting plant, but when we arrived, Luba's scarf was saturated with blood. I was taken immediately to the examination room. The doctor on duty examined my hand, and said something in Russian to a nurse. Then he cleaned my hand with an antiseptic solution.

Now I could see the wound for the first time. The left finger was a bloody mess; it was split open to the bone and swollen to twice its normal size. The doctor demonstrated what he wanted me to do by moving his index finger back and forth. I tried to follow his example — it was slow and painful, but I could move the finger. The tendons, apparently, were not damaged. The doctor examined the back of my hand, pressing the knuckles while I moved my finger. This procedure was extremely painful and concluded the examination. Hand and finger were bandaged, then put into a sling. I was given two tablets for the pain, and the doctor tried to put me at ease, saying,

"Don't worry. Your finger will be all right."

Ludwig and Alexei were called in for the usual red tape. The doctor asked Alexei how the accident occurred. He said that he did not know, as he had arrived too late. With my limited Russian, I tried to explain; I avoided mentioning Kostja's name.

"*Choroscho*. I'll try to write my report from what you said."

Then the doctor turned to Alexei,

"See that the prisoner is properly conducted back to camp."

Alexei looked about helplessly, sticking out his lower lip, as if he were going to spit. He asked if Ludwig could escort me back to the camp.

The doctor was undecided. Going to the telephone, he asked to speak to the guard.

"It's all right, but Alexei will be held responsible for both of them."

The doctor passed this message along.

I was helped into my fur coat; the doctor made me put my hand under it for protection against the cold.

At the guardhouse, Alexei had to sign a paper. Before we parted, the "Spitter" stuffed some tobacco and paper into my pocket, spat on the floor, and said softly,

"The winter is long and cold. Take your time." Speaking to Ludwig, he said, "Take him back to the camp!" Then he turned around, abruptly leaving the guardhouse.

When we reached the camp, the officer on duty asked, "What's the matter, 'Jena'?"

I pointed to my bandaged hand, and said, "Stupid accident."

"Go to the clinic where the Novotnik expects you."

Lidia Novotnik greeted me with an icy look. Her eyes appeared so suspicious, my blood almost froze in my veins. At last the Goddess of Vengeance said,

"What's the matter with your hand?"

"I've had a freak accident."

She rose, walking a few paces towards the window, appearing to be more interested in the snow crystals on the glass than in my hand. She turned suddenly,

"How did you do it?"

As she bored her eyes into my face, I shrugged my shoulders. I seethed with disgust and had to be careful not to say anything.

"Go to Dr. Meinicke in the hospital at once. I'll be over there shortly."

I was glad to get away from her.

I made a complete report of the accident to Dr. Meinicke, who nodded his head, going to work right away. He had no sooner loosened the bandage when the Novotnik strode in. Both of them examined the wound which had almost stopped bleeding. Dr. Meinicke disagreed firmly with the Novotnik about the treatment. He insisted that the finger should have been stitched and put into a straight resting position immediately. Of course, she disagreed with his opinion, saying,

"It's quite all right as it is."

I sat through this argument near fainting. Hours had passed since the accident, and the agitation, pain, loss of blood, and the constant rumble of my empty stomach, left me in a state where I just didn't care anymore.

Finally, my hand was bandaged again and I was given a bed. Since all the hospital beds were supplied with straw sacks, one could sleep like a child in its mother's lap. Outside the hospital, only a small group of people could boast of such luxury.

I had to be awakened for the evening soup which I ate hungrily. Later, visitors came to see me. Rohdenbach said that a little rest could not hurt me and promised to bring me something to read.

Of course, Peter and Ludwig dropped in too. Peter asked if there was anything he could do for me.

"Certainly," I answered, "Tell Heini Kuhnert I like my eggs sunnyside up."

Peter winked, "I'll do that, Kurt."

Strangely enough, in all the years of our friendship, he never once called me "Knüppel". When Ludwig and I were alone, our conversation centered on our work.

"Say, Knüppel, as you know, I don't like this Russian garble, but I do understand quite a bit of it."

"Really?" I asked.

"Your report didn't mention anything about Kostja, did it?"

"I didn't think it would make any difference one way or the other."

"Why not? It was his fault, wasn't it?"

"I think that he was just a bit careless. But I'm sure it was an accident."

Ludwig agreed, "Perhaps you're right."

"Should anyone ask you stupid questions tomorrow

at work, tell them you were behind the box and didn't see it."

Ludwig nodded, leaving with the promise to return.

It was about 10 o'clock that night when Heini Kuhnert appeared. Most of the other patients were already asleep. He handed me a pot full of kascha.

"Eat, Woman", he said, "You've got to keep your bust line."

He did not have to tell me twice, and I stuffed myself like a cannibal. I barely finished, when he grabbed the pot, rising from the bed.

"Do you have anything to smoke?"

"Yes."

"Good. I've got to return to the kitchen. I'll be back tomorrow night, if I can't come, I'll send someone else. All right?"

"Sure, Heini, thanks."

"Button your lip about this, okay? See you!"

Heini disappeared as quickly as he had come.

CHAPTER NINE

The days passed and Christmas drew closer. I was satiated with sleep and *kascha* by this time, and I shared my good fortune with Ludwig. He told me that the "Tovarisches" at work often asked about me. Luba in particular was concerned. Once she sent me half a newspaper and a pack of *machorka* through Ludwig. (Russian newspaper was used as cigarette paper.) Kostja and Alexei, the Spitter, also looked after my smoking pleasure.

"Do you know, Knuppel", Ludwig said, "For several

days Kostja ran around like mad, but when he found out that he wasn't held liable for your accident, he reverted to his old ways. He still loves his daily nap and just can't stand the sight of work."

The hospital life appealed to me more each day, because outside the wind blew its icy blasts at the working brigades. From inside the hospital, we heard the sound of the snow crunching under stomping feet. And the wash brigade was probably worrying about where to find the wood for the hot water they so desperately needed.

What a dog's life! Here in the hospital, I waited for breakfast, had a soft bed, and could sleep until doomsday. I did not have to worry about norms and nariats, wind, cold and snow. Yes, sir! This was the life. Even an inside toilet had been built for the hospital. Selfishly, I told my conscience to shut up!

Actually, I was afraid that my finger might heal too quickly, and secretly I bent it every day, so that the wound would stay open. The Novotnik expressed her dissatisfaction with my progress and ordered my entire arm be put in a resting position again. I had the feeling that Dr. Meinicke knew about my finger exercises, but he never let on.

Once in a while, Dr. Meinicke invited me up to his office for a chat. He loved to talk about show business and was extremely interested in our theater group. I felt that he liked me and put a trust in me which I valued highly. I learned much about his private life, his professional life, and many aspects of camp life that were not public knowledge.

I drew up a schedule for my time in the hospital. Several hours were spent studying Russian; Peter gave me a daily lesson, then I studied alone, preparing for the next day. I memorized many Russian words this way, but the grammar still remained a mystery.

One day Spiess Wiegand dropped in, and solicitously asked if there was anything he could do for me. I thanked him saying, "Sorry, I just can't think of anything right now."

He was astonished, and lifted his eyebrows, saying, "I'm glad you have good friends."

In the course of their rounds, the Antifa, in the persons of Finke and Wetzlaff, came to the hospital. They tossed around big words, and even bigger plans for the future. Both wore the brass "A" on their chests. They sat on my bed, discussing the theater group with me when Finke let the cat out of the bag.

"Knüppel," he said, "In the next production, you're going to have the chance of a lifetime to prove you really have talent."

Curious, I asked Finke to continue.

"It's going to be a comedy, and you'll portray the daughter of a rich plantation owner in South America. Knüppel, this could very well be a smash hit. What do you think of it?"

"Well, let me read the script and I'll give you my answer."

Through the interest shown me by the camp celebrities, my status rose in the hospital, and some of the hungry patients swarmed around my bedside to get a share of my leftover food. Others obviously resented me and treated me with coldness.

Despite their aloof attitude, I was surprised to receive an invitation to one of those neurotic feasts Wilhelm had described to me. Out of courtesy I accepted, bringing some *kascha* and bread with me to the table. I was finished eating before those characters had even started, and ignoring the disgusted looks they gave me I rolled myself a cigarette. Wilhelm was right; it was disgusting! Also, I never received another invitation.

After curtly saying goodnight, I returned to my bed and lay awake thinking. Since, to us Germans, Christmas is the most joyous and intimate festival, I wondered if there was some way I personally could make a contribution. I was thinking about building a bridge between the patients and home. How, and what, depended mainly on the support I could get from certain individuals. A conversation with Dr. Meinicke fell on fruitful ground; he promised to give me his complete support. The Antifa also liked the idea, implying at the same time that they had been the first to think of it. Rohdenbach promised to supply music and Heini Kuhnert promised to do his part. The ball was rolling.

I told none of the patients about our plans. Christmas Eve came and the Christmas Spirit was at a low ebb. Dr. Meinicke walked through the hospital, giving a short but moving speech. Then came the first surprise when Heini entered carrying a pail of soup and one of *kascha*. The gift was well received. However, I noticed that the gourmet club members saved the vegetables out of their soup for later. They were incorrigible!

Cigarettes were lit and we all wished one another a better Christmas next year.

I was glad to see the tongues slowly loosening and hearts opening up. Then came the culture group, with Finke, Wetzlaff, and Rohdenbach leading. The conversation died down, and faces expectantly turned to the Antifa leaders. For about an hour we patiently endured speeches filled with best wishes, promises of improving present conditions, future plans, and, of course, "home transports". We were saved from further torture by the abrupt arrival of Spiess Wiegand.

He wished us all a Merry Christmas. The musicians took the opportunity to play "Silent Night, Holy Night", "O Tannenbaum", and "O, Dufroehliche." Everybody joined in singing. It was a touching moment, one of inspiration and thoughtfulness.

We sang many more carols and the hardened and emaciated faces now carried an inner glow of peace. When the music stopped, and the vibrations of the last note were still in the air, one could hear a pin drop. Then came the handshaking, and clearing of throats, while many prisoners fought down their tears.

The Russian people don't celebrate Christmas when we do, and the brigades had to work the whole Christmas Season. Then came New Year's Eve when most of the hospital patients were in bed sleeping. Only a few of us sat around the table talking of punch and poundcake. We had been given a little *kvass* with the evening meal, and with this we toasted a better year to come. *Kvass* is a bitter tasting drink which as far as I remember was made from water and yeast and pressed vegetables, etc.

In January the thermometer continued to drop and it became mercilessly cold. Even in the hospital we could feel it. My finger now began to cause me more concern — the wound was healing. I asked Dr. Meinicke about it. He told me not to worry, that I would remain in the hospital for the rest of January at least. That put me at ease.

Rohdenbach brought me my script and I began to study it. Clearly, much was expected of me; a rich, spoiled, young woman was quite an undertaking for my limited talents.

After two weeks, I had the script memorized and began to focus on the personality. The first rehearsal date was set, and I received permission to be there.

At the beginning of February, I was released from the hospital and for one week performed light duties around the camp. Then I rejoined my old brigade; it was a memorable day when I returned to Schitz.

Everyone was nice to me. Alexei, the Spitter, offered me tobacco for one cigarette but gave me enough for three. Kostja sacrificed his daily nap for my sake and tried to act ambitious; but he could hardly keep his eyes open. I thanked Luba for her concern and for the tobacco she had sent me. She smiled, revealing her even, white teeth, and said, *"Nitschewo."*

One night, shortly after I returned to my place at

Schitz, Peter entered Barracks 8. Looking important, he said,

"Kurt, the G.P.U. wants to see you right away."

Uneasily, I asked him why. All he said was,

"Burgajeff and Schwefel want to see you. That's all I know."

Lieutenant Schwefel, the G.P.U. and liason officer of Camp 6/10 greeted me jovially. He invited me to sit down, speaking to me in German.

"How's your hand doing?" he asked, conversationally.

"It's progressing nicely, thanks."

"Good." Lieutenant Schwefel said. Then suddenly the Russian work officer interrupted, speaking Russian. He said that Schitz was adding more people — four lathe workers, two mechanics, and four men for general labor. He felt this brigade had grown large enough for its own brigadier.

"You were recommended to me from two sources for this position. Also, you seem to be able to communicate in Russian rather well. Do you think you can fill the post?"

I was greatly relieved and also surprised, but thinking quickly, I answered,

"It all depends on how much you expect me to do, sir."

Burgajeff seemed pleased with my reply, and nodded,

"As brigadier you'll be completely responsible for the work performance, behavior and production norm of your men. In other words, keeping everybody happy, and bringing me good nariats!"

Still undecided, I looked to Schwefel who smiled, and added jokingly,

"Yes, Jena. It's going to be a real task for you. You'll have to be a diplomat; if that doesn't work, use your feminine charm!"

Both officers chuckled, amusedly.

"Can I have a probation period?" I questioned.

"Permission granted!"

With that I was dismissed. Peter waited for me in the next room.

"What's the story?" he asked impatiently.

"I've been made a brigadier." I answered, still thinking about it.

"That's marvellous, Kurt! Good luck."

"Thanks, Peter."

I returned to the barracks and told Ludwig what had happened.

"You're rising in the world all right." he said, "Strike the iron while it's hot!"

"That's right, Ludwig. But don't forget one thing."

"What's that?"

"In prison one has enough problems filling one's stomach."

"I'm sure as a brigadier you'll have the best chance of doing that."

"I don't deny it."

"So what's your real problem?"

"As a good brigadier, you must be concerned with the stomachs, lives, and health of your men. It comes automatically with the position; I know that from the 'Wehrmacht'. The same pattern will apply here, too."

Ludwig reflected for a while, then said,

"Look, Knüppel! All over the world, there are the leaders and the followers, the rich and poor, and the smart and stupid. You must choose which class you'll belong to."

I rolled myself a cigarette and thought some more about it, while Ludwig added,

"Knüppel, I've wanted to say this to you for a long time, and I might as well spit it out now. Ever since your stage success, you've been fighting with yourself and it's ripping you apart."

I looked at him, surprised.

"Let me speak," he continued, "As your friend, I can't help seeing the signs of this inner battle. Even in your sleep, I've caught you talking about it. Why Knüppel?"

How well he knows me, I thought!

"If you promise not to laugh at me, I'll try to explain."

"Shoot!"

"Just like yourself, I thought I knew the rules and regulations of our camp. I despised the nobility, the profiteers, and the position-seekers." I looked to Ludwig for confirmation; he noded, then said,

"Go on."

"Since my stage success, everything's been going too fast for me; I can't adjust to it. I feel as though one foot is on the shore, while the other is in a boat moving out to sea. Which foot should I withdraw? In their Words, . . ."

"Save your breath!", Ludwig interrupted, "I understand you very well. However, you must make a decision for your own good. You can't go on tormenting yourself."

"I'm glad you understood, Ludwig. The question remains, which foot must I pull in?"

"Only you can be the judge of that; but don't forget one thing."

"What's that?"

"Don't bite the hand that feeds you."

Peter appeared with the names of the men in my brigade.

"Here," he said. "Bring your men together; they're all going to live in Barracks 8."

I looked over the list, and counted, besides myself, sixteen men.

Peter related the news that tomorrow there would be twenty-five men coming from Camp 7/10. Then he dashed off again.

I gathered my men together at Barracks 8, then I submitted their names to Onion Head, Krauskopf. Most of us now accepted Krauskopf like a disease one tolerates because one must.

My first day as brigadier was quite exciting. Hardly had I arrived at the plant, when I was called to the office of the *Natschalnik*. Tovarisch Skutovitch, the man who never smiles, received me reservedly. He regarded me with a rigid expression on his face. In uniform today, he paced the office with his hand in his pockets down to his elbows. Alexei was present too, looking as if he was nailed to the floor. Natschalnik Skutovitch suddenly stopped, and regarded me, saying,

"Brigadier Stock, I hope you realize the importance of your new position. I expect you to inspire your men to surpass production norms. You must set an example for them. Since they all work under one roof, I have informed the camp administration that you too will take up an earning position in our production plan." He continued, "Alexei has received his new duties, and you will take over his shop regarding the handling and delivery of materials from the smelting plant. Besides that, you're responsible for the cleanliness, and disposal of scrap. Alexei recommended you as his successor. I was doubtful so prove that I'm wrong."

Natschalnik Skutovitch lit a tailor made cigarette, and said,

"That's all, any questions?"

"Yes — one. What happens to Kostja?"

I looked at Alexei; he thought for a moment, then said,

"From now on, he's under your command."

I thought immediately of Kostja's sleeping sickness, and was determined to remedy it. Tovarisch Skutovitch told me a few more things, then dismissed us. I had not understood everything he said to me, but I was very sure I would!

Once outside, I had a thousand questions to ask Alexei. All he answered was,

"Come on, brigadier. We've got lots of work to do!"

All in all, it was a memorable day. Before the month was out, I was so deeply involved in my work, I almost forgot I was a POW. I discovered something I had not believed possible under these conditions, my sense of accomplishment at the end of the day's work. Life began to take on meaning because my work so preoccupied me, I did not have time to think about the hopelessness of my situation. After work, my time was spent with the culture group. From morning to night, I was caught up in a schedule that demanded so much from me both physically and mentally that my inner torment left me. I ate when and where I could, taking every bit of food gratefully, and without shame or scruple. The pillow on which I rested had an invisible slogan: "He who gives is entitled to receive."

In the course of the following months, Kostja and I became friends. I had some success, too, in curing him of his sleeping sickness. I discovered the key to his indifference to life quite by accident. While we waited for the iron at the smelting plant, he told me something about his childhood.

"Where's your home, Kostja?" I asked.

He spread his arms in a wide circle, saying,

"Mother Russia!"

"Where do your parents live?"

"I have none. I was raised in an orphanage, and shunted from one place to another. They slapped and kicked me all over Siberia."

Suddenly, I understood that neither force nor empty promises could stir his ambition or build his hopes. I was sympathetic to him, which led me to the right approach — to give Kostja the feeling that somebody cared.

One day, while the work was in full progress, Kostja was missing as usual. As I expected, he was sleeping behind the furnace. I sat down next to him, and asked him if we were still friends. He sat up, blinked, and said yawningly,

"Certainly. Why do you ask?"

I cursed, and stood up, saying I felt that friends didn't abandon one another when the going was rough.

"But that's all right." I said, "Go back to sleep, and I'll do all the work myself."

It was not long before Kostja carried iron as if he were making up for lost time.

The comedy, *"Verwirrtes Herz"* (Bewildered Heart) was another smash hit. Now the acting talents of the entire cast really came to the surface. I, as the spoiled daughter of a rich father, had a role which demanded versatility and the camp newspaper said I had exceeded all expectations. In one scene, for instance, I had to cry lustily. I surprised myself by shedding real tears at every performance. "Bewildered Heart" had a long run, and I must confess, it was a wonderful feeling; an intoxicating success as well as a satisfied stomach. My position as brigadier was also a source of great satisfaction though it was somewhat limited by prison conditions. I had more freedom of movement being no longer confined to a single place, and I used this advantage for all it was worth.

The transporting of the iron from the foundry to our place of work was now solely my responsibility, and I slowly made friends with the crane foreman. I was able to procure for him some of the small items that were made in the camp, and because of his gratitude, I was able to deliver the iron to Schitz in record time. Alexei was puzzled by the speed with which I did this, and showed his appreciation by giving me tickets from his ration card for the Stalowa, the messhall.

Everything ran smoothly as in a well-oiled machine. I was only a tiny wheel in the entire operation, but I knew how many little wheels were essential to the entire production.

Slowly, I began to understand that there actually were people who regretted the end of the war. To them, the war was the biggest gold mine known to man. Civilian society could, with a good deal of justice, be compared to our camp life. There was the class structure, the daily struggle for survival, and the greed for profit.

Here is an example, which I can cite from the various accounts I collected over the years as a prisoner and soldier. Every man engaged in battle or front line duty requires nine men to supply him with munitions, food, etc. This line of supply stretches all the way from the front lines to the munitions workers back home.

The front soldier is content merely to have enough ammunition, rations, and a pair of clean socks in his duffelbag, while an unteroffizier, only twenty kilometers behind the front, in charge of a saw-mill, is king of is own domain. Everyone needs building materials, and many of the supply units try their best to keep the unteroffizer in a good mood. One hand washes the other, or live and let live — business flourishes and everyone is happy.

Further back, let's say fifty kilometers from the front, sits a sergeant-major at the desk of a supply depot. He is in charge of the divisional supplies, and sends the best cigarettes, liquors, and delicacies to the proper people. A secure position, a "K.V.K., First Class" (a good conduct and achievement medal), and extra furloughs are not things to be despised. The further one goes behind the front lines, the larger grow the cogs of the tremendous war machine.

I learned that entire boxcars filled with coffee, cigarettes, and chocolate had disappeared without a trace. I discussed these things with other soldiers, and we speculated about the culprits in these masterful robberies. Once, while we sat around talking about these things in camp, a private commented in a voice filled with bitterness.

"What a shame! It appears that I've shot my ammunition in the wrong direction!"

The bitter cold slowly began to abate, but the death toll continued to rise. The pitiless Siberian Winter wrote the bill and the Grim Reaper came to collect.

For a while there was some talk about "going-home-trnasports", but we soon realized that prisoners were merely shuffled around from one camp to another.

Around the beginning of April, the cold weather broke, and the temperature rose noticeably from morning until noon. The sun sent down its warm rays partially melting the snow. But the night frost came, and an occasional snow fall; this brought doubts about an early spring. Finally around the middle of April, the snow really began to disappear, and our fur coats became too warm to wear, and our felt boots, useless; they soaked up the wetness like a sponge. The *Banja* (delousing station) worked around the clock to dry our boots, but was unsuccessful. Finally, each of the barracks built a ring of scaffolding around the furnace to dry our boots which improved the situation somewhat; but whether in the Banja or the barracks, getting one's boots in the morning was a miserable ordeal. There was a general scramble for boots, and one had to be really lucky to find his own pair; often he'd find himself with two right or two left boots in his hand.

Thank God, this period did not last too long because at the end of April, we were issued summer clothing. The prisoner in charge of the clothing room, as a token of his enthusiasm for the theater, gave me a pair of leather shoes. They were patched and repaired many times, but I held on to them; they were much better than wooden ones or gummi-galoshes. For my head, I was given a brown hat that looked something like a ski cap. There were only two such hats in the entire camp. Later, because of it, I was put in an embarassing situation.

With the change of season came a reexamination and reclassification of the prisoners, and transfers in the working brigades. As Ludwig and I had feared, we were put back into Group 2 again. I was lucky; the work officer reinstated me as brigadier. The Novotnik was against it but she finally relented. Ludwig, however, was sent to the smelting plant. We both spoke to the Antifa and others, but they could not change the order.

The next morning, I went to the foundry for Schitz's. I looked around for Ludwig, and to my astonishment, I discovered him in the notorious rear-axle production group. This brigade was called, the "Devil's Brothers" or the "Devil's Brigade". They were so named because in Hell conditions could not be any worse. The work was exceptionally heavy, and a wall of fire on two fronts created an inferno.

The rear-axles were shaped and stamped out by powerful hammers, and from there they went to an enormous press. As they left the press, they were seized by three of the "Devil's Brothers" who could not carry the 110-pound shaft very far, as another one waited for them immediately. They dumped the axle on the floor and hurried back to catch the next one, and in no time at all, a wall of fire built up behind them. And in front of them was the tremendous heat from the furnaces. Prisoners in this brigade collapsed like flies, the murderous heat dehydrating their bodies, they sank to the floor from exhaustion, heat prostration, and lack of moisture.

They suffered first and second degree burns and were continuously being sent to the camp hospital. There was a constant need for replacements, because even if a prisoner on this brigade was lucky, and escaped being roasted alive, it was only a matter of time before his strength became dissipated, making him unproductive.

However, there was one Lucifer who made a name for himself on the Devil's Brigade. He was a rugged prisoner from Bavaria who survived the tortuous labor, incurring no serious burns. He worked as if he had never done anything else in his entire life, and he outlasted all the other men on this brigade, becoming eventually promoted to hammer leader. He received the undivided respect and admiration of the Russians as well as the German prisoners. After 1947, when we were paid for our labor, he earned maximum wages as a prisoner (150 rubles a month).

I stood for some time watching Ludwig work, he was bathed from head to foot in sweat, panting heavily from the heat and the fast pace of the work. My God! I thought, how can a man go on like that all day! That evening, when Ludwig returned to the barracks, he was more dead than alive. I wore down the heels of my newly acquired shoes trying to have him transferred. I sought out Spiess Wiegand, Rohdenbach, and others who promised to do their best for Ludwig. But all their efforts were to no avail, and for the time being, Ludwig remained in the pit of Hell.

CHAPTER TEN

May Day is the biggest holiday in the Soviet Union, next to the celebration of the October Revolution.

Banners, flags, and enormous pictures of Stalin, Molotov, Lenin and other personnages looked down at the marching masses of workers. Youth organizations and other groups carried slogans such as: "Work and Bread", "The Youth of the Free World March Together", and "Victory Over Capitalism".

In Camp 6/10 we also participated in the celebration. A podium had been constructed for the occasion and Major Bogoslaw stood there, delivering a long speech. He reminded us that it was a great honor to work on the rehabilitation of Russia and to be part of the struggle against capitalism. The words "work", "freedom", "rehabilitation", "glorious struggle", and "eventual victory", were reiterated constantly. In recognition of their distinguished work, ten prisoners were called to face the assembly. One was the prisoner from Bavaria who worked in the Devil's Brigade, he was the first to be called. While the ten stood at attention before the podium, they were proclaimed the outstanding workers in Camp 6/10, and given a vacation. For two long weeks, they didn't have to leave the camp, and could sleep as much as they wanted, provided their empty stomachs let them.

After thirteen days at the smelting plant, Ludwig joined the rank of the casualties coming from the Devil's Brigade. He and two others were carrying an axle from the press when one of his partners dropped his tongs, and the heavy, red hot axle crashed to the floor on

Ludwig's foot. Dr. Meinicke diagnosed two broken toes on his left foot, and when I visited him in the hospital he was delighted to show me his cast. We smiled conspiratorially at one another. Ludwig had a superstitious nature, and believed that the number 13 had played a mysterious role in his accident.

The beautiful May weather brought noticeable alterations in the appearance of the camp. The camp brigades were busier than ever, filling the main street with gravel, digging deep latrine ditches and giving all the barracks liberal coats of white wash — the Russian dirt and bug eradicator.

Everywhere could be seen prisoners of war sitting on their barracks roofs, looking nostalgically into the distance. The barbed wire, the high palisades, and the machine guns, were powerless to contain our thoughts. The spring weather nurtured a disease against which we were powerless; even Dr. Meinicke, with all his knowledge, could do nothing for us against this disease home sickness.

Sporadic groups of prisoners came together and shared their memories of the homeland. While imprisoned, I travelled mentally with my buddies to various places, in Germany, getting to know them almost as well as if I had actually visited them. I strolled through the Black Forest, skiied in Bavaria, and picked Erika in the Lüneburger meadows. In Hamborg I shouted "Hummel, Hummel!". Greeted people with "Servous!" in Vienna and searched for amber on the shores of Palmnicken. But my heart beat twice as fast when I thought of my native Berlin. There, to stroll Unter-Den-Linden, is as beautiful as the lyrics of the famous song describe it. I greet you, my Berlin the city whose magic no one can escape. I remembered my birthplace, as it was in the days before the war: the Wintergarden, with its dome of glistening stars, the Mokka Efti with Erhard Bauschke at the microphone, the Skala with "Doorlies-Tropical-Express", the Kurfüsten Damm, the Berlin Zoo, the Gedâchtnis Church. And I can never forget the crowds of people from all over the world during the Olympic Games in 1936. The athletic competition, the merging of all peoples, fostered the ideal of peace on earth. That was my Berlin, as I remembered it.

The flames of escape were ignited again, fanned by the spring breezes. Small wonder that some would rather face death attempting to escape, than wasting away in prison. The chances of success were slim, as we all knew. Most prisoners played with the idea, but almost all dismissed it under the pretext of waiting for a more propitious time.

One day, around the middle of May, the incredible news spread through the camp that three men had actually made the attempt. What was most astonishing, was that one of them was Otto, the wheeler and dealer from Berlin. The whole camp was in an uproar, and the Russian command reacted quickly to discourage any further attempts. A search was immediately conducted, and several prisoners were interrogated.

In the hospital, I discussed it with Ludwig; neither he nor I had as much as a suspicion of Otto's plans and none of the others suspected anything, either. I gave Ludwig some tobacco and paper, and inquired about the food situation.

He said, "When you see Heini tell him that my foot is in a cast, not my stomach."

"I'll attend to that immediately, anything else?"

"That's all I can think of for now."

I walked quickly over to Barracks 25 where Heini was just leaving.

"Where are you going?" I asked.

"To the latrine."

We walked silently, together, and afterwards sat on the grass, talking for a while. I asked him directly,

"Do you think that Otto's going to make it?"

"Hard to tell. He promised to send me a postcard from Berlin."

"That's very considerate of him."

"Listen, Knüppel." he said, "Let's stop beating

around the bush, I gave Otto my word not to discuss it —
for the time being anyway."

"Good enough for me; you must keep your promise,
let's drop it for now."

"One thing I will say", he continued, "Is that guy has
a lot of guts, and the heart of a lion."

I switched the subject, delivering Ludwig's message.
Heini asked me how he fared.

"Poorly. Yesterday when I visited him, he was so
hungry he chewed on a piece of his cast, and now he's got
indigestion."

Heini grinned, promising, "Don't worry. I'll look after
him."

Days passed and the tension in the camp increased.
We were all anxious to know about the escape; naturally
our best wishes went with them. But after a few days, the
two prisoners who had escaped with Otto were brought
back. Severely beaten, with a bloody face and swollen
eyes, they were held before us as examples. Then they
were thrown into the camp prison. Like zoo animals,
they were kept there as an attraction for a week. Then one
day they disappeared, no one knew where; Russia is
vast and full of mysteries.

Heini now thought it safe to talk to a few trusted people about Otto's escape. Apparently, he had used the two
as decoys. While they headed west, Otto set his sights for
India. Still the wheeler and dealer from Berlin.

We were diverted by the arrival of forty new prisoners,
among whom were a violin maker and two new performers. Alfred Hirsch was a melodious baritone who
had sung opera, and was on a first name basis with many
famous people. The other was Horst Laube, a drummer
of exceptional ability. Both of them were from Berlin.

But the greatest surprise was yet to come, one of the
new men went to Spiess Wiegand, declaring Paul Finke,
the president of the Antifa, was an imposter and a swind-
ler. He told the following story:

"Paul Finke and I belonged to the same unit and

fought in the last days, defending Berlin. Somehow Finke disappeared without a trace; he was listed as a deserter."

The prisoner finished, "I don't like to denounce others, but this man lives like a big shot, telling lies about concentration camps that would melt a stone. I can't stomach it, besides I'm morally obligated to my comrades under the ruins of Berlin."

Spiess Wiegand called together the executives of the Antifa, and Finke was put on trial. Rohdenbach was the prosecutor and Wiegand, the judge. The key witness was concealed behind the stage curtain. Of course, Finke denied the charges, tried to belittle them. But he changed his tune, when his former "comrade" stepped forth, pointing a finger at Finke, and saying,

"He is a deserter and a liar."

Finke was crushed under the weight of the evidence. He was a pitiful sight; with an ashen face and whining voice, he begged for mercy from the court. Under cross-examination, the fraud came to light.

After Finke had deserted his unit, he changed into civilian clothes, and under cover of darkness, he swam the canal and surrendered to the Russians. Finke told the G.P.U. officer that he was a Communist of long standing. The Russians were doubtful, sending him to Siberia just to be sure. Then on the transport, Finke made several important changes in his story, claiming he had been freed from a concentration camp by the Red Army, and was being sent for re-schooling as a prisoner of war. His stories seemed to ring true, which were not surprising because he had direct information from his cousin, who was a guard at Auschwitz. Once in Siberia, he managed to convince Wetzlaff, and together they began organizing the Antifa with Russian support.

In the course of the trial, Welzlaff was called in and cross examined, too. Despite skillful questioning, he remained in the clear. There was no choice but for the Antifa to report the shameful situation to the Russian command. The G.P.U. was furious, and Finke was thrown into the brig. That was salvation because I am convinced that he would have been torn to pieces if we had gotten hold of him.

However, there is no doubt that this was Rohdenbach's golden opportunity. He now became a political leader as well as cultural director for the camp, climbing another rung in the ladder of prestige and security. This man, with an unsatiated thirst for power, adopted me, and for the time being, my fortunes rose with him.

The G.P.U. persuaded the Antifa that a good theater program would go far in boosting the morale of the prisoners, and turning their thoughts in other directions. Given the chance, Rohdenbach was more than willing to show the Russian command his capabilities.

First came the outdoor chess board with the 60 centimeter pieces. A tournament was arranged, and the Russians were delighted to participate, facing tough competition from some of us.

Next on the agenda was the variety program. Under the slogan, "Musical Showcase", the first rehearsals began. Rohdenbach conceived and constructed scenery that was really extraordinary. Since Ludwig was still in the hospital, our tango was dropped. The addition of Alfred Hirsch and Horst Laube enriched our theater group considerably. Alfred took us by storm, and Rohdenbach, magically, produced two drums from his bag of surprises. Horst played them unusually well, and stole the spotlight. We sat enchanted, tapping our feet to his dazzling rhythms.

Then I came on with my new number, "Aphrodite in the Tub". It was a silhouette act wherein all the movements of a woman bathing were parodied, and projected onto a linen screen by a powerful light. The effect was remarkable, and while I went through my act, Horst Laube accompanied me on the drums, singing a catchy tune. At the curtain call, we received a standing ovation.

A few days after our opening performance, as I returned from work, I saw Peter waiting for me. He immediately broke the latest news,

"Guess what's happened, Kurt! Last night the supply barracks was broken into!"

"That's incredible! Did they catch whoever did it?"

"Not yet, but the G.P.U. is working on it. They're conducting interrogations right now. The camp was thoroughly searched this morning but no evidence was found. That's all for now, Kurt. I'll keep you informed."

Peter hustled off.

After the roll call, I went to the culture barracks to get ready for the night's performance. Peter came rushing in; out of breath, he said I was to go to the G.P.U. immediately.

"What's the matter, Peter?"

"Search me, Kurt. I don't know."

Schwefel received me coldly, following my motions with searching eyes. I had the uncomfortable feeling that all faces present, from Captain Purka's to Spiess Wiegand's, were hostile. I knew this atmosphere all too well — cross-examination. Every muscle was tight with apprehension, and every nerve was tense as Schwefel addressed me as "Stock". This was already a bad sign because he had given me the nick-name "Jena".

"As you probably know, the supply barracks was broken into last night, and we have already obtained confessions which leave little doubt in our minds. Why did you do it!"

There was disappointment in his voice, as he continued to stare at me menacingly.

I answered curtly, "I had nothing to do with it."

"Lies will further endanger your situation; you were seen yesterday in the area of the supply barracks. Somebody recognized you by your work cap."

I looked to Spiess Wiegand for help, but not a muscle moved in his face. Probably, he had been ordered to keep his mouth shut.

"Lieutenant!' I went on, "I swear I had nothing to do with the break-in. Yesterday after the evening roll call, I went to the culture barracks to prepare myself for the performance. I did not leave the barracks for several hours. After the performance, I sat with Rohdenbach and Westzlaff and we discussed several minor changes in my act."

Westzlaff and Rohdenbach were summoned immediately, and both confirmed my alibi. Schwefel did not give up though,

"And what did you do after the performance?"

"I went to my barracks, falling asleep soon afterwards."

"You expect me to believe that?"

"Certainly, its the truth!"

Spiess Wiegand asked to speak.

"Lieutenant Schweful, it has occurred to me that there is someone else who wears an identical hat."

Schwefel looked undecided while Rohdenbach took advantage of the opportunity to support me. He too asked for permission to speak on my behalf.

"Lieutenant Schwefel, I give you my word, that the charges against our Knüppel are absurd. He has worked closely with me all week and I promise, gentlemen, that if you can prove he is guilty, then I will go voluntarily to the "Devil's Brigade.""

Schwefel whispered to Purka, then, staring directly at my face, he said,

"Stock, evidently you have good friends; but, it appears, you also have enemies. I am going to review the evidence against you."

With that I was dismissed.

The next day the entire camp was assembled for an investigation by the G.P.U., with police dogs. After the dogs had caught the scent, they were led up and down the rows of prisoners. They were stopped before each man and allowed to sniff him. My heart must have missed several beats when the dogs stopped before me. Finally, to my indescribable relief, the dogs continued down the line, and close to the end, they began barking loudly. Three men were identified and immediately led away;

later they were put in the brig with Finke. I learned that the next day, when all four had been led out of camp under heavy guard, loaded into a truck and driven away.

Around the end of June, again there were signs of a transport. Ludwig was the first to pass the rumor along to me, saying that the Novotnik was making a "clean sweep". Anyone who could still crawl was dismissed from the hospital and put to work. Ludwig was written up as 3/6 and sent back to Schitz.

To the great disappointment of many, only the incurables, the crippled, and those completely incapable of work were listed for transfer.

The transport was loaded with the sick from the camps surrounding Tscheljabinsk. Hardly had it departed, when a replacement of about seventy able-bodied men arrived to fill the gap. From these, three new men were added to the theater group; each, was a personality in his own right.

"Traber-Karl" (Also nick-named "Baron von Münchhausen") was a Berliner who loved horses. Apparently he had been raised on mare's milk, because he knew every racetrack, jockey, and naturally every horse that had ever raced. He also bored us to tears with endless stories of his amorous adventures with rich women from home and abroad he had met at the race tracks. Rohdenback listened patiently through all this; but to judge from his face, one would imagine he had just bit into a lemon.

"Pretty Albert" was a cook and caterer by trade, and soon worked in the army garrison, cooking for the officers. He spoiled them with all sorts of exotic dishes. His position gave him great freedom, special privileges, and of course, first class eating. Albert was as much a master on the stage as before a stove. He could sing, tap dance, and was something of a selfstyled "Houdini", and he did everything well.

Bubi Reich was the third performer, he had studied speech, dancing and acting at the Alexander Golligen School; this was an excellent recommendation. In a short time, he had Rohdenback were involved in discussing the technical details of the theater.

The qualifications of these men fitted in perfectly with Rohdenbach's grandiose plans, and a new program was planned, called "Vienna Blood". The most famous songs of Vienna were planned to move the hearts of the audience. Then the first rehearsals began.

The Siberian summer is short but very hot, also the lack of humidity makes the midsummer heat bearable. The climate, however, is deceptive; a prisoner who worked outdoors, contracted a sunburn of unusual severity, and he lay in the hospital critically ill with a high fever, and large blisters on his back.

The Black Brigades at Kapasys had by now become accustomed to their work and production went smoothly. Yet accidents, continued to take their toll. A prisoner was killed instantly when he was struck by a piece of iron which slid off a load of bars the crane carried overhead.

There was a prisoner who became an expert on the power saw. His superiors praised his work and wrote him good nariats, but perhaps he had become too sure of himself because while he was pushing hard to fulfill the super norm, his hand slipped, caught on the rotating blade and was torn to ribbons.

Another prisoner, working the night shift, was caught in the engine of the plant locomotive. He was delivered to the city hospital, suffering from internal bleeding.

The Devil's Brigade still roasted, and was constantly in need of replacements.

My respect for the Russian women grew from day to day. They wore the same rough work clothes as men, and worked side by side with them. They carried stone and mortar, and were as capable with the welding equipment as most women are with the household iron. I saw women piling up wood, pulling heavy wheelbarrows, even carrying rifles, as they guarded the plant gate.

Once, I asked Alexei, the Spitter, why the Russian women did such heavy work. He looked for a target, then spat before he tried to explain the situation to me.

"In Russia, every man, woman and child must help develop this country of ours." Then he voiced the time-honored dictum, "He who does not work, shall not eat."

I tried to defend our Western European women, reminding him that women have other duties more important than slaving alongside men-folk, or for that matter, running around with guns.

"What for example?" Alexei, condescendingly.

"Oh, raising children, for example."

Alexei interrupted me by waving his hand,

"Your women-folk are pampered too much!"

I asked in what way.

"Let's say that a German woman is pregnant. Four months or so before the birth of the child she leaves work, and her every whim is catered to." He took a deep breath, continuing, "After the birth, the same pampering continues, and goes on for several months. This woman is useless for at least a year, contributing nothing to the production and development of your country. Now, our women here!", and his voice lifted with pride, "When they are pregnant, and their time comes, they leave the factory on their lunch hour, go home, give birth, and return to work before the lunch hour is over!"

Alexei looked at me triumphantly, rolled himself a cigarette, and walked away, leaving me standing there, dumbfounded.

In the summer of 1946, the theater group performed for the work detachment outside the camp; we travelled by truck sometimes as much as forty kilometers. These detachments worked all summer on the collective farms, and in some cases, lived there all year. They were isolated completely from the main camp, except for rare occasions.

It was a beautiful summer's Sunday when we left the camp. After traveling for about two hours, we reached the collective farm where our comrades worked. The detachment had 68 men, consisting of a cook, tailor, shoemaker, and barber, who also tended the sick. The command leader was Sergeant Thiele. The detachment lived in a hut which was separated from the village by a ridiculously low fence.

Apparently our coming was no secret because the entire population was assembled to meet us. Singing, we rode into the village and were joyfully greeted. At once, I noticed the prisoners were shabbily dressed, but appeared to be in good health and well fed. Later, when I spoke with some of them, I learned that the main complaints were the lice, diarrhoea, the workload, and the complete isolation from the camp. The civilians and guards treated them pretty well. Strangely enough, there had not been a single escape attempt. I asked one of the prisoners how they fared with the local girls. Winking slyly, he reported,

"Certain girls give lessons in Russian," and he shoved me in the side.

I understood the innuendo. Ludwig shrugged his shoulders and speaking like a school master, complained,

"My Russian is miserable! I could use some lessons myself!"

To our surprise, our comrades had set up an open air stage, and it appeared the entire village would be our audience. Children were running around while expectant eyes were looking impatiently at the stage. The girls wore colorful skirts, silk kerchiefs, and giggled.

Lieutenant Schwefel gave a speech in both languages. Next, the music began and the inspiring march, "Alte Kameraden" warmed up the audience.

Everything went perfectly; today, under the blue Siberian sky, we could do no wrong. We improvised freely to our hearts' content while our grateful, unsophisticated audience gave us overwhelming applause. Traber-Karl and Pretty Albert seemed to be especially inspired by the presence of so many local beauties.

After the performance, Pretty Albert tried to inveigle one of the girls into showing him the livestock in the stables. Lieutenant Schwefel caught onto Pretty Albert's enthusiasm for farming, and said simply, *"Njet"*.

We were given a hearty meal and afterwards there was singing and dancing with the peasants. It seemed as if the entire village took pride in serving us.

As with everything else, even this special day of my life as a prisoner of war ended. When we left the friendly people, many hands waved, "dozwidania". The village elder, a tall man with a white beard and kindly eyes, thanked us in the name of his people. He bid us good-bye, saying, "Come back soon. You've brought us much happiness today."

The truck rolled on, accompanied by the melody of a sad folksong. It lingered in my ear for many kilometers, and was so appropriate to Russia and her people. All in all, it was a beautiful day, and a peaceful one for us prisoners.

In the summer of 1946, we had two more opportunities to visit outside. We looked forward to them, and to this day they are vivid in my mind.

The summer came to an end, and "Vienna Blood" was on our usual high level. It brought melancholy to every music lover in camp. With regret, I found myself supplanted by a rival, Bubi Reich; he also played a woman's role and was the sensation of the camp. With proper modesty, I must admit Bubi was eminently suited for the part. His figure, movements, and even his voice, overflowed with feminine charm. Pretty Albert and Bubi Reich danced a Viennesse Waltz that would have pleased Herr Strauss himself. To the great disappointment of Ludwig and myself, they also danced the tango, "Jealousy". But it must be admitted, they were overwhelming and could have performed on any stage in Germany without shame.

The potatoe harvest was past and winter was not far away. For two weeks, I moved into the hospital because an abscess the size of a tennis ball had developed on my left elbow. Before the operation, I was in considerable pain and couldn't sleep nights. After Dr. Meinicke had opened the tumor, I was once more able to enjoy the straw sack and the preferential treatment. My only regret was that it had not happened in winter.

To everyone's surprise, the entire camp was issued straw sacks, shortly before the bitter winter of 1946 set in. There was great concern over the political situation and talk of war. The propaganda mentioned poor relations between Russia and the Allies. Our hopes for release were further away than ever.

The second Christmas in prison arrived, while the Siberian winter surrounded us with its snow, cold, and the pitiless east wind. The culture group visited the hospital with a small program, as in the previous year. As we walked along the camp street, the snow crunched under our feet and the frost bit into our faces. We were going to comfort the sick, and had the best intentions of bringing them courage, hope, and a little piece of home. Truly a worthy undertaking, but who was inspiring us, the missionaries of hope and good-will? Would we sink completely in the hopelessness, the lack of freedom, or the debasing environment? Who gave us courage and inspiration for our heart aches? No one!

I was able to speak with Alfred Hirsch about many things after one of our performances. He told me his life story and I was deeply moved by the misfortunes of this talented artist. His was a life full of disappointments, and his story reminded me of another great singer, Joseph Schmidt. It is generally known that artists are high strung and very emotional, and in all probability, Alfred Hirsch suffered more than the average prisoner under prison conditions. He suffered not only for himself but for everyone. But his sensitive heart could give only so much because he devedoped a serious heart condition, and in the summer of 1947 was sent home. Never will I forget his farewell performance. By popular demand he sang, "Rede Pagliacci", while tears ran down his heavily powdered face. After my release in 1949, I visited Alfred, becoming acquainted with his family. In his spare time he sang for small gatherings, churches, and hospitals hoping for a chance to resume his career. However, life did not give him that opportunity. In 1950, Alfred died in a hospital in West Berlin, broken in body and soul. He was a good friend, endowed with a heavenly voice, but died in deep poverty and disappointment. The curtains were drawn, the lights dimmed: "Rede Pagliacci".

January and February passed; but the winter continued unabated. It held us in its claws and tore great gaps in our ranks. There were continuing cases of frost bite and work accidents.

Since the arrival of Bubi Reich, his rocket-like prominence began to affect my popularity. To top it off, Rohdenbach called me into the offices of the Antifa, coming without hesitation, right to the point.

"Knüppel", he said, "Since you are well-liked and respected here, I've been giving some thought to your future. How would you like to be my right hand in Barracks 8, as a reschooling officer?"

I looked at him amazed.

"Well, how about it?"

"I'm so overcome, I don't know what to say!"

"I hardly need remind you that the position will be a respected one; you must take this opportunity."

"I'm well aware of the importance of such a position, August."

"So? What are you hesitating for?"

"For one thing: I feel I'm doing enough for the Antifa culturally, and I had the impression that everyone was satisfied with my services." Rohdenbach was going to interrupt me, but I said, "Wait a minute, August, let me finish. I believe that each person should do the work he's best suited for, and I'm afraid I couldn't be much help to you politically."

"Why not?"

"I'm not competent to lead others in a political sense, since I'm confused, myself."

Rohdenbach looked at me suspiciously, and enunciating each word carefully, he said,

"In other words, you are not anti-fascist?"

"Let's put it this way, August, I'm a pacifist."

He threw up his hands in despair.

"We don't see eye to eye!"

"Very well," I added, "If you will force my decision now, August, that's fine with me. I believe I would be incapable of doing any political work at present, because I have not yet developed any strong political opinions."

Rohdenbach paced nervously back and forth, finally, stopping before me; he poked his finger at me, saying in a restrained voice, "Knüppel, I can't force you, but I must say you disappoint me very much."

"I could say the same about you, August!" Somehow the words slipped out.

He regarded me, more surprised than angered.

"What do you mean by that?" he asked finally.

"Nothing in particular, August. But remember this: *Nicht der ist dein Freund, der alle deine Taten gutheisst!*" (He is not your friend who always praises what you do.)

I turned toward the door, and since no retort came, I quickly left the Antifa office.

May Day, 1947! As previously, there was fair weather, and Major Bogoslaw made another long-winded speech. We were lectured on the remarkable agricultural progress the Soviet Union had made since the war. Of course, the prisoners of war at Camp 6/10, had done our duty conjointly with the Russians. On these grounds, Major Bogoslaw continued, it was a great pleasure for him to give the outstanding workers of Camp 6/10 two weeks' vacation, and to my great surprise, my name was called out.

Ludwig bragged to the workers at Schitz about the honor I had been given. When I returned to work, they all called me, "Stachonowski", jestingly. Since I had never met the gentleman, I asked Alexei about him.

He explained that Stachonowski was a worker, surpassing all other workers. He was a model, and a symbol of the perfect norm, a man, who because of his magnificent work, was praised from one end of Russian to the other.

When I related this story to Ludwig, he said, mockingly.

"I'm proud of you; from now on I'm going to call you "Stockonowski"!

The idea spread through the camp, and soon everyone called me "Stockonowski!"

Luba Czernikow was one of the few who was deferential to my position, giving me a big piece of bread, a cooked potatoe, and a smile that made me dizzy. The rumor went around the plant that we were madly in love, and when it reached my ears, I just smiled and said nothing.

To our general astonishment, a surprise commission came from Moscow. It was composed of several officers, and led by a major. He was a tall, well-built man, with a handsome face and stern eyes, wearing a custom-made leather coat. He was, truly, a figure from a magazine. Our sobriquet for him was "Leathercoat". He apparently, had the full authority of the Russian government behind him because his orders were curt and their execution was precise. His excellent German befitted his appearance. Leathercoat, followed by his officers, visited our barracks asking many questions. The prisoners ahd waited a long time for such an opportunity, and answered unhesitatingly. To the question, "When was the last time you were given tobacco?", the answer humorosly came at once, "March, 1945, in the German Wehrmacht!" Leathercoat cut him off with an icy look, then asked us detailed questions about our working hours, food, cleanliness, and clothing. Then he permitted us to ask questions, and from many voices in unison came, "When are we going home?"

Leathercoat showed no trace of surprise; however, he hedged with his answer.

"I can't give you an exact date for your return; but I

can promise you this much, the 'Home Transports' are already started."

This statement was much analysed and dissected by us later. Ultimately, we felt no wiser than before. Another prisoner asked,

"Herr Major; when will we be able to write home?"

Leathercoat smiled. Then he looked at us, without apparent deceit, and said,

"Tomorrow. I've brought Red Cross postcards with me."

Hurrah! was the answering shout. The commission left the barracks, going directly to the kitchen. As Heini Kuhnert later informed me, it was as if a tornado had hit the place. They snooped around, turning everything upside down in their thorough investigation. Complaints fell profusely — the finger-nails of the staff were too dirty, and the flour too white; the cook was too fat, and the soup too thin. A Russian officer stood next to the soup kettle trying to count the fish eyes as they surfaced. After the inspection, the head cook was demoted, and sent to the Black Brigade, while Heini Kuhnert was promoted to chief cook. From that day on, orders were issued to clean the fish before putting them into the soup!

The next target of the commission was the hospital, and Dr. Meinicke was especially happy about their arrival. Before he could speak, he had to listen to their abuse first. But, as a good doctor, he knew how to swallow a bitter pill. Finally, he was permitted to air his views. Once he got going there was no stopping him, and the Russian officers wrote everything down. Dr. Meinicke had many complaints, and a barrel full of wishes. The Novotnik tried to interrupt him several times, but the hand of Leathercoat demanded silence from her, and authoritatively, he said,

"Let Dr. Meinicke speak; you will have your chance later."

The Novotnik was insulted, and silently she kept in the background.

Leathercoat kept his promise; the next morning we

received postcards. We were all happy and excited. God
be thanked! At last we could establish communication
with our homes so far away. Each of us found a little
privacy, where we opened up our hearts and wrote to
our loved ones.

The climate in Camp 6/10 was good; in fact it was
extraordinary. So far, Leathercoat's coming had brought
us one good thing after another. Overnight, he became a
legend. Peter told me some more about the devastation
left by the commission that had turned the administration
building into a shambles.

"Believe me, Kurt, there's a big storm on the way!"

Peter was right, the events of the next few days was
simply unbelievable. In the beginning we heard only very
few details, but slowly a clear picture emerged. The
commission had discovered that the books had been tam-
pered with: embezzlement!

Several people were interrogated and among them
was Lieutenant von Bulow. Apparently, what they learned from him was very informative. Under guard, he was
led out of the camp and we never saw him again. There
were rumors, though, that he was the key witness in
court. True or not, the fact remains that later many of
the officers (including the camp commander, Major Bogoslaw, the administration officer, and the G.P.U. chief,
Purka) were replaced by others.

The commission did not forget the Antifa because
Leathercoat was dissatisfied with their program. He insisted on broader rehabilitation activities. This made the
puppets jump, beginning an intense political drive. The
obviousness of the scheme was embarrassing. Rohdenbach and Wetzlaff canvassed all the barracks, spouting
tirades, empty promises and big words. Rohdenbach
especially could have fooled any gathering of party comrades with his monumental enthusiasm. His lust for
power equalled his pleasure in hearing his own voice.

Finally, he became so intense, he did not realize that
his methods had a negative result with most of us. He

pushed too hard, was too loud, and in general, he was not very convincing. Like myself, there were many who wanted a new political outlook but patience, time and trustworthy guidance would accomplish that eventually. We had had our fill of cheap promises in the past.

CHAPTER ELEVEN

At the next medical examination, the Novotnik spent more time than usual in examining us, particularly those in Group 2. Apparently she sought men in the best physical condition, and according to her judgment, Ludwig and I were good enough for the Olympics. We didn't know the reasons for this procedure, but the rumor was that we would be sent to the lead and coal mines. This time the latrine talk had come closer than ever; the next day, we learned that a work detachment was being assembled for stone quarry work. At the same time a "Going-Home-Transport" was being selected, causing the whole camp to be in an uproar. Finally, the names were released, and Ludwig and I learned that we were headed for the stone quarry! The following reminded me of the army:

Orders were issued in rapid succession to keep us from thinking. Meanwhile, Peter sailed into our barracks, handing a list of names to Onionhead Krauskopf. All out of breath, Peter climbed up to our bunk without wasting any time.

"Instead of you two just sitting here twiddling your thumbs, you could do something about this stone quarry business. What's the matter with you both?"

"What do you suggest, Peter?" I asked.

"Why haven't you gone to the Antifa?"

"Cut it out, Peter! The 'Antifa' knew even before our names were on that list."

"What do you think, Ludwig?" Peter asked.

"It's hard to say, we'll see."

"I've got to go, now. See you later, okay?" Peter dashed off.

Krauskopf read off the names of those who were to report to the culture barracks immediately. Besides Ludwig and myself, 19 others were called, and the total stone quarry detachment numbered 76 men. Our leader was Guenther Nagel, while Emil Mueller was in charge of the kitchen. Both men were recent arrivals to Camp 6/10, and I did not know them personally.

It was June 14, 1947. Lieutenant Schwefel addressed us with these words:

"Men, you have been chosen to work in a stone quarry. The work is hard and it requires enthusiasm and a certain amount of skill to do the job. Those are the main reasons why you were selected; we had no choice but to select the best workers of Camp 6/10. Remember one thing; your conduct will be taken into consideration when the time comes for repatriation."

Next was Rohdenbach's turn to say good-bye to us, and sure as hell, he gave us an even bigger line than Lieutenant Schwefel did.

Ludwig's reaction was: "Knüppellowski! You did the right thing by not accepting the political position that son of a bitch offered you."

"I'm glad you see it my way, pal."

Muttering to himself, my friend murmured,

" 'If one is born to be hanged, he will never be drowned.' "

Rohdenbach and Wetzlaff did everything possible to justify themselves, to Ludwig and me.

"We did everything we could to get your names off that list!" Rohdenbach groaned.

Wetzlaff rushed to his support, "Believe me Knüppel; the Russians are very touchy now, and their ears are closed to all suggestions."

"Sure, we understand," I said. To spare us more of this, Ludwig and I wished them good luck.

We were awakened early the next morning, while two men went to the kitchen for food for the quarry workers. As in the army, we were ready to go long before the trucks arrived. Peter dashed in to say goodbye; the thought of separating from him was heavy on my heart. I would have loved him to come along with us. However, I convinced myself that my big brother role had lost its meaning because Peter had grown up and did not need me anymore. According to the unwritten law, a soldier does not allow his feelings to show, and with dry eyes, as tears flowed in my heart, I grabbed Peter's hand.

"Take care, Peter, and keep your eyes open. Don't forget to keep in touch. Send us a message whenever you can."

"Will do, Kurt." Peter croaked, hoarsely.

"Keep alert, Peter!" said Ludwig, laying his paw on Peter's shoulder. "Don't forget your friends, and if you're pressed for time, just send a carrier pigeon along."

Peter smiled at Ludwig's wit. Another hand shake, then Peter tore himself away from us, running up the barracks steps to ground level and disappearing from sight. Ludwig watched him leave, and partly to himself, said,

"I'm sure going to miss that blue-eyed monkey."

"You took the words out of my mouth; I can't stand good-byes", I said, "They're always the same. Each tries like the devil to hide his emotion, and there's a lot of empty talk which is meaningless."

I was weeping. A friend had walked out of my life, a friend who had given me so much without question. There was no way I could put a value on what Peter had meant to me during the long, hard months in prison camp. I would always remember him.

The work brigades left the camp, and finally, three

trucks arrived to transport us. Spiess Wiegand assembled us before the barracks, making us stand at attention, straight as a razor. Then he gave his report to Lieutenant Schwefel who called out the name of each prisoner. As each man heard his name called, he climbed into the truck. The second truck was reserved for provisions, kitchen supplies, and tools. Finally, a few guards climbed into the trucks with us.

When everything was ready, the signal was given to leave. The trucks rolled through the gate very slowly, and we were reminded of the inscription overhead: "He who does not work, shall not eat."

When the last house of Tscheljabinsk faded into the distance, we turned north and went cross-country for about an hour and a half. Suddenly, as if sprung from the earth, a small settlement appeared on the horizon. The convoy stopped before the entrance of a small prison camp; it was our destination. An old civilian guard, with an antique rifle, attempted a military salute. Lieutenant Schwefel thanked him, then went quickly towards a man in civilian clothing. We were told he was the *Natschalnik* of the stone quarry. The order to debark from the trucks was given. We formed ranks, and were officially turned over to the command of the new camp. From the appearance of things, the event was very important, because everyone acted with great formality; even the old civilian guard appeared conscious of history, as he shortened the strap of his blunderbuss. The *Natschalnik*, a giant of a man, stood before us with legs slightly spread apart. His stern eyes inspected us unsympathetically; his square jaw jutted forward, and his voice rasped like sand-paper.

"German prisoners of war, my name is Andrej Movka; I am the *Natschalnik* of the stone quarry you will work in. I expect two things from you — work and more work. You will soon find that I'm harder than any stone in the quarry when it comes to work." He went on, "That's all for now. You can break formation while the command leader takes over from here."

Later, Guenther Nagel informed us that the first shift started at 8:00 in the morning, and the afternoon shift, at 6:00 p.m. We spent the rest of the day doing routine work — grounds clearing, scrubbing the barracks, etc., and we were overjoyed to discover straw-sacks on the bunk beds. Except for Nagel and Mueller, who had a room for themselves, we all slept together. The water for the kitchen was brought in by horse and wagon from a well outside the camp — two huge barrels were used to transport the water. Ludwig and I were sent to the well. On the way, half respectfully and half teasingly, I saluted the guard. To our surprise, the honorable Red Army veteran stood at attention and gripped his shoulder strap. Our military discipline paid off in dividends later because Petrov became our staunch ally.

Ludwig and I were able to slip away from the grounds work to take a look at our surroundings. The camp was fenced in with a palisade of seven foot wooden posts without barbed wire. It impressed me more as a trappers' fort than anything else. Ludwig looked at me questioningly,

"It doesn't make any sense," he said, "Escaping from here is as easy as stealing candy from a baby."

"Yes. And I'll bet you a pack of Machorka, Petrov would look in the opposite direction, too."

"You could be right at that, Knüppel. Everything looks too easy. There must be a catch somewhere."

Our inspection was interrupted because it was time for the evening soup. After our meal, the entire detachment was assembled and taken to the stone quarry which was about five minutes away. Looking into it, was like seeing a bomb crater. From all directions, railway tracks ran like a spider's web, while turning platforms connected the tracks and tilting lorries stood in a long row waiting to be filled. As Natschalnik Movka explained it, two men or more would work on each track, and the norm per man was five lorries filled with stone, gravel or sand. Movka pointed with his finger at the lorries, emphatically stating, "Each man *must* fulfill his norm!"

Later, back at the camp, the shifts and the brigades were assembled. Ludwig and I were put on the day shift, working on Track 3. Our brigadier was named Paul Jellinek. The strong ones among us were selected, and were assiged to unload stones from the quarry onto the main track of the railroad. These men would perform the heaviest work of all.

The track builders were the only professionals among us. They had worked on the German railroad, and later in Russia, under the motto, "Wheels must turn for victory".

On the 16th of June, at 7:45 a.m., the first shift went to work taking the tools from the pump house at the bottom of the quarry. With more good will than know-how, we stumbled to our tracks. Ludwig and I brought an empty lorry over to Track 3, then stared bewildered at the stone face before us. There was no stone, no gravel — just plenty of sand. I glanced over to Track 4; there were plenty of stones. Our neighbors were hammering away unmercifully at a big rock, they sure meant business. Their blows came rapidly, full of rehabilitation spirit.

But their strength ebbed quickly under the murderous speed, and exhausted, they leaned on their hammers. With red faces, puffing heavily, they stared at the small pile of stone splinters they had chipped off. Two other comrades attempted to retrack their lorry after it had been derailed.

The *Natschalnik* hurried from track to track, giving advice and orders. When he came to us, we pretended to be working with enormous industry, scratching in the sand like chickens. Distrustfully, Movka regarded our empty lorry, then us. Scratching his chin, he said,

"When you finish digging your garden, don't forget to put the sand in the lorry."

The Natschalnik turned to Guenther Nagel who stood beside him.

"Those two field mice must work better than that, if they expect to eat!"

Movka noticed the comrades on Track 4, trying again

to break up that large stone block. With quick steps he strode over to them, gave the rock a professional glance, took the hammer from a prisoner, and split the block with a few well placed blows.

"That's the way to do it." Movka said, handing the hammer back and stepping nonchalantly over to another track. He was followed by an awe-struck Nagel.

Around 12 o'clock, the work siren screeched; by that time we had filled two lorries with sand. Our work place looked like it had been swept with a broom. The heros of the morning were the crew from track number 7 who had three lorries filled with stones and one with gravel. When our relief man of Track 3 asked about our progress, Ludwig said dryly,

"Someone must have concealed our stones; we're still looking for them."

The rest of the shift, my partner and I worked very hard, accomplishing nothing. After we had filled one lorry with gravel, there was nothing more we could do on track 3, so Jellinek put Ludwig and me onto another track. A Russian stone driller moved to our track and began drilling into the stone face, then the railway men appeared extending the track closer to the wall. Around five o'clock, the signal blasted and it was suppertime.

After the evening meal, we gathered around, talking about the work. We decided more experience was needed for this kind of work. Jellinek stressed that for now, good will, team work, and organization could help us to fulfill the norm satisfactorilly. As we became more experienced, the work would become easier. Everything he said was plausible and intelligent.

For the next two weeks our inexperience and clumsiness with quarry work were dearly paid for. Injuries, mostly of a small nature, were a daily occurrence. I was no exception, and as souvenirs from this period, I still carry scars. Gloves were seldom distributed, but when they were, they rarely lasted more than one shift.

Despite all of Emil Muller's efforts to feed us decently,

all of us were emaciated. On Sundays, Emil did his best to surprise us with something which he would concoct from the meager rations allotted to him. He was a real chef, and a good, person, besides. Guenther Nagel promised us that nothing would be taken from the kitchen on the sly, and extra duty in the kitchen and camp, were rotated as a matter of course.

Brigadier Jellinek conscientiously aided us during those difficult weeks. Because of him, we finally reached the point where we could fulfill our daily norms. With all our strength sapped from us, we stumbled back to the camp, tired, but with a sense of accomplishment. The hunger and craving for food, was never so overpowering as it was in those summer months of 1947.

Our camp command, including Movka, was aware of the seriousness of the situation in the camp and reports demanding replacements went to the main camp. Shortly afterwards, the Novotnik, Schwefel, Wetzlaff, and Rohdenbach arrived. The Novotnik examined the parade of skeletons, apparently surprised by the pitiful physical state we were now in. Looking at us with a stern face and compressed lips, she touched our hanging, rear ends. On this day, 15 men were sent back to the main camp and written up as 3/6.

When I talked with Wetzlaff, he gave me a package of Machorka and greetings, both from Peter. He was about to go, when he said,

"Ach, I almost forgot! Peter gave me a message for you which he wanted repeated word for word: 'Silvertooth hasn't changed. He's still in love with his sticks.'" Wetzlaff looked at me for enlightenment.

To satisfy his curiosity, I said it was an old joke between Peter and me, and I tried to laugh as though it were very funny. Wetzlaff wasn't convinced, but just then he was called away by Lieutenant Schwefel.

As soon as Wetzlaff was out of hearing range, Ludwig asked me to tell him the joke. I explained to my friend, it wasn't a joke, but a message in code from Peter.

"You don't say!" Ludwig said.

I told him about Frankfurt and Tovarisch 'Silvertooth'. Ludwig was silent for a while, then finally, commented, "It must have been terrible."

"It could have been worse; I got away with my life."

"I still don't understand", Ludwig continued, "What 'Silvertooth' has to do with the message?"

"It's as clear as day; the interrogations are continuing in the camp, accompanied by pressure and torture."

Ludwig nodded his head understandingly, adding, "Peter is not as naive as he looks."

Wetzlaff suddenly lifted his arms high in the air, as though praying to the sun.

"Listen, everyone! Lieutenant Schwefel has just informed me that on the next suitable Sunday, the culture group will be here to visit you."

Somewhere in the back, a voice shouted, "Don't forget to bring along some extra food; it's hard to laugh on an empty stomach."

Several prisoners applauded the idea of having some emotional stimulation. The majority, however, thought first of their stomachs. Wetzlaff was unperturbed, and with a conjuring motion, he lifted his hands high again,

"I . . . I promise you a Sunday full of excitement, comedy, laughter, and a bag of surprises."

Someone next to me moaned, "I'd love to have this guy with me for one shift on my track; I'd give him all the excitement he'd need."

Late that afternoon, the high and mighty rolled out of camp, taking the prisoners unfit for quarry work with them. Ludwig and I sat outside on a bench, smoking silently, each of us preoccupied with his own thoughts.

"Knüppel", Ludwig broke the silence, "Did you feel that Wetzlaff couldn't make a move today without Lieutenant Schwefel following him?"

"Well, yes, since you mention it — but it might have been a coincidence."

"Possibly, but I had the impression that Schwefel tried

to prevent Wetzlaff from saying anything about conditions in the camp."

"You could be right, Ludwig. Right now, though, I'm not very interested — what worries me is where can I find something more to eat."

"You're right, Knuppel. We've got to do something about it, if we don't, who knows what the consequences will be."

He looked at me questioningly.

"If you think I'm going to try to ruin my health like those guys back in camp, then you're nuts. I've already lost so much weight I hardly throw a shadow, standing in the sun. In case a transport is ready to take me home one day, I'd like to survive the trip."

"I agree, pal; I just had to find out your intentions."

Early Tuesday morning, the train waited to be loaded with the stones piled up along railroad track. Our brigade was on the day-shift. We were split up; the men on Tracks 5, 6, and 7 stayed in the quarry, and the drillers were able to choose their locations without any interruptions because the quarry was almost deserted.

The train consisted of 27 open cars, two-thirds were to be loaded with stones, the rest with gravel poured in from a conveyor belt. The stones had to be loaded manually, and the norm was 20-tons per man, or two men for a 60-ton car. Ludwig complaining about these cars, said, "Those piss-pots are as big as battleships."

The loading work was supervised by Gunther Nagel who offered a bonus. If a man finished his norm before the shift was over, he could return to camp. Ludwig and I were assigned to a 60-ton car that was not merely a battleship — it must have been the Bismack itself! Luckily, we had plenty of stones on either side, piled up to the rim of the car walls. After we managed to lower the side walls, we began throwing small and medium sized stones into the middle, placing the big ones on the edges. The sweat poured down our bare chests, and we worked without let up. A little after 2:00, the job was finished! Mov-

ka personally inspected our car, and gave his *Choroscho*.
Then Ludwig and I returned to camp.

Apparently, Natschalnik Movka was pleased with the
performance of the first brigade because he smiled often,
seeing how well we progressed. The train was loaded and
pulled out, and the second brigade started their shift after
a good blast. They were busy as bees, and Movka was in a
good mood. The next day he informed us that from now
on a prisoner could leave the quarry as soon as he fulfilled
his norm. Everyone was elated at this announcement.
Apparently the *Natschalnik* realized what it would take to
double our efforts.

But this advantage concealed corresponding disadvantages. We clawed at the stone like possessed men; the
crews competing to be the first to finish; bitter warfare
raged between the two brigades. Jellinek tried his utmost
to maintain the spirit of unity in our brigade, but it was
useless. The spirit of competition was too strong.

Track number 7 was the undisputed champion; its
crew always left earlier than the others. Apparently they
had bragged too much and went home too early because
Movka put a damper on their own self-glorification. A
third man was added to the crew, and now they had to
fill 15 lorries per shift to meet their norm. Our track number 3 was generally considered the worst track in the
quarry; we carted away more sand than any of the others.

Luckily, my friend Ludwig was adept in handling the
shovel. I was somewhat better than he at breaking stones
and handling the hammer, and eventually I developed
quite a good technique. Despite the fact that we worked so
well together, we still had a tough time fulfilling our norm.
Certainly, even we had bonus days when we returned to
camp early, but this was mostly after a good blast. Often
we had to scrape our last two lorries of gravel from neighboring tracks where the crew had already left.

Some crews quarreled among themselves constantly.
Since the inception of this murderous piecework, the work
was dominated by selfishness. Jealousy and ill-will

abounded everywhere; most of the prisoners lived by the pronouns, "I, me and myself".

In the meantime, the reinforcements from the main camp had arrived. On the average, they were in better shape; a few, almost fat. There were some peculiar types among the new arrivals. One man boasted he was a cooper by trade and that he was expert at swinging a hammer. On his first day at work, he acted as though he would satisfy all our norms, singlehandedly. No one could tell him anything, and his first attempt de-railed a lorry filled with gravel. After that, he picked up a hammer and began to show everyone the proper way to break up stone. He banged strenuously, but hardly made a dent. Disgusted and deflated, the expert regarded his hammer as if it were the guiltry culprit. We named another prisoner, "Cousin" because he always addressed everyone by this name. Cousin used to work on the city market, and could talk faster and longer than any one. We were frequently amused by his mile-long speeches, but the funniest thing about him was his face. He had small, sly eyes, and bushy eyebrows which met on the bridge of his nose. A nose which was uniquely oversized. Once I said jokingly to Ludwig,

"When the Lord gave out noses, Cousin must have yelled, 'Here!' twice!"

"No doubt." Ludwig replied, "As they say, 'It looks like the scythe the farmer leaned over the fence'."

At last, the desperately needed barber came to camp. Our Figaro was not only a hair and beard cutter, but also the medic. His renowned skill as a barber, and the know-ledge he had gathered as an army medic, were most useful. It was not too long before this enterprising man had a thriving business among the civilian population, both as a barber and a general practitioner.

The reinforcements brought a wagon load of news from the main camp, they told us, that the Russian camp commander, Bogoslaw, the work officer, Burgajeff, and the G.P.U. officer, Purka, had all been replaced. There was a trial in which Manfred von Bulow played an important role. We were further told that a large building project was underway; new barracks and a hospital were being built. Leathercoat had shown up unexpectedly at the camp again, his visit was short but effective.

Since the last medical examination, the food situation had improved somewhat. The soup was thicker, and we received a piece of fish daily. On Sundays, Emil Muller even prepared something like a menu for us. We loved Sundays, when we went to the sauna, received clean underwear, and did not work. That is, if a train didn't arrive. The high point of the day, however, was the afternoon meal.

It was the first Sunday in August when around 7:30 we were awakened by the most dreaded of all sounds, the locomotive's shrill whistle. Our worst fears were realized, the brigade which had to load the train, would have its Sunday ruined.

As the job fell to the second brigade, we in the first, acted rather smug. While the comrades in Brigade 2 cursed like long-shoremen, the locomotive piped merrily as it was being transferred from one track to another.

Cousin was the first to complain, "I've always hated to work on Sunday ever since I've gotten into the habit of having breakfast in bed."

Cousin's bunk neighbor, lay on his back with his hands folded over his chest. His voice vibrated as he recited a verse from the Bible, saying something about Sunday rest. He did not have a chance to say "Amen", however, for Guenther Nagel walked suddenly into the room, demanding silence.

He said, "Listen, all of you. This train was not expected until tomorrow. Unfortunately, today is when the culture group is scheduled to arrive, too. Emil and I had decided not to tell you because we wanted to surprise you. But, as you can see, *der mensch denkt, doch gott lenkt.*" 'Man discloses and God disposes'." Nagel continued, "There is a way of helping the situation — who from the first brigade will volunteer to help?"

For a moment, it was so still, one could have heard a pin drop. Then someone volunteered — Brigadier Jellinek climbed down from his bed, saying,

"You can count on me."

As he began dressing, Ludwig peered from his upper bunk,

"Knüppel, are you awake?"

"Who in the hell can sleep in all this commotion?" I growled.

"Do you think we should help those poor buggers?" he asked, loud enough for everyone to hear.

"We might as well, or they'll never get done!"

Ludwig appeared to have been expecting an answer like this, because he jumped out of his bunk with so much enthusiasm he almost hurt himself. His willingness to help broke the ice, and from all directions men climbed out of their beds and began dressing. Cousin sacrificed his breakfast in bed, and while he dressed he bored us with one of his endless orations.

His neighbor, even though grumbling about the lack of respect on the Lord's Day, followed the example of everyone else.

The second brigade cheered us for our helpful attitude, and together we hurried to breakfast. In the meantime, Natschalnik Movka showed up. Except for Mueller, our cook, and a sick man, the entire command, laughing and clapping each other on the shoulder, moved towards the train. Natschalnik Movka shook his head in wonderment; he probably never had seen such happy workers.

That Sunday demonstrated what comradeship and unity could do; the train was loaded in four hours flat and ready to leave. Triumphantly, we returned like gladiators back to the camp. Deep in our hearts was the knowledge there still existed something besides homesickness, hunger, cold and lice — comradeship!

The culture group arrived at one o'clock, and by this time, we were practically starving. The artists received a hearty welcome — Rohdenbach was the first who jumped from the truck, then followed Traber Karl, Pretty

Albert, Bubi Reich, the Viennesse duo, Gruber and Kronenberger, Kohlmeyer and several others I didn't know. One face was hidden in the background — it was Peter! With a mischievious smile, he sprang to the ground. Happy with his surprise, he pressed my hand with so much strength, I thought it was in a vise.

"Peter! You old so-and-so, how are you?" I blurted out joyfully.

"Good, and how are you both?"

"So-so, friend." Ludwig answered, shaking Peter's hand warmly.

"Say Peter, have you become an artist too?" Ludwig asked curiously.

"Aren't we all hunger artists?" he replied.

Ludwig looked at me with raised eye brows.

"Schwefel invited me to come along even before I could ask him."

The magic words, "Chow time" ended the discussion. The meal was eaten outdoors, on benches and tables built by the prisoners who were here before us. Our cook outdid himself and the food was delicious. Unfortunately, there were no second helpings. As we smoked, Lieutenant Schwefel gave us the usual speech. He tried to be brief, but mouthed a number of beautiful phrases as an extra dessert. Finally, he said,

"Your work performance has improved greatly, and your conduct as prisoners is excellent. Natschalnik Movka has praised your leaders and industry. Don't slacken now, let me remind you again, that your efforts will be considered when the time for repatriation comes. Also, if you keep up the good work, the culture group will come again. I wish you all a happy time."

Rohdenbach greeted us in the name of the Antifa, and surprisingly proceeded directly with the program.

A stirring march, opened the show, and shortly afterwards there was humming and singing. The spirit was free, the weather beautiful, and the stomach satisfied;

we had a good time! Days like this were very special and rare, for quarry workers in particular.

The performance reached its finale, with the song, "Happy Days Are Here Again" whole-heartedly sung by everyone. The culture group bowed and we showed our gratitude with unceasing applause.

Before our guests left, Ludwig and I tried to speak further with Peter. Needless to say, we overwhelmed our friend with endless questions. When we came to the subject of "Home Transports", Peter smiled, embarrassedly.

"Don't be so secretive", Ludwig said, "Say that we two handsome fellows are leaving on the next transport."

"What good will that do, since none are leaving?" Peter replied, sidestepping the subject.

Rohdenbach, Traber Karl, and Pretty Albert came over. Traber Karl tried to be funny, saying to me,

"Knüppel, I must confess, that fully dressed, with long hair and a bust, you looked much sexier!"

I ignored his attempt to needle me, and I addressed Rohdenbach,

"August, do you have anything sensible to say?"

"Well, everything's pretty much the same Knüppel. Old faces go and new ones arrive. You may be interested in knowing that a building project has been initiated; we'll be getting new barracks, a new hospital, and a completely renovated culture barracks."

"Aha!" Ludwig interrupted, "That's why there aren't any home transports."

"What's that got to do with it?" Rohdenbach grumbled.

"Why, it's as clear as black ink." Ludwig continued, unruffled, "Ivan isn't putting up all that money for nothing. Do you really think he's building a brand new nest to send us home?"

"Perhaps the barracks aren't being built just for us?" Pretty Albert suggested. Before Ludwig could think of a good retort, our comrades from the culture group were summoned to the trucks. We shook hands quickly, and said good-bye. They ran to the trucks where Lieutenant Schwefel waved impatiently, and clambered up. The truck slowly rolled out to the tune of "Auf Wiedersehn".

CHAPTER TWELVE

The potato harvest in our section of Russia begins in early September, and is a time not only of hard labor, but of much rejoicing and thanksgiving. I was aware of the devotion with which the potatoes were handled, and once I asked a Russian why the potato harvesting was surrounded by such reverence. He answered,

"As long as the Russian people have potatoes in the cellar and bread on the table, we are thankful."

We would soon discover for ourselves the truth of this statement.

During the harvesting season, Russians came to the camp from all directions asking for helpers. At first Natschalnik Movka was reluctant to let us work outside on our own. When he finally approved, Guenther Nagel vouched for each one of us.

About half the men on the idle shift were allowed to work outside, helping with the harvest. Ludwig and I worked for a Volga German named Alex Schmidt; he was not unknown to us, because he worked as a mechanic in our gravel mill. Besides a small, well-kept garden, Alex owned two fair-sized potato fields which the three of us worked, while his thirteen-year old son drove the horse and wagon.

At twelve o'clock, his wife called us to lunch, Alex was amazed at our tremendous appetites. Our break was over as soon as we finished our cigarettes, then we returned to the field. At three, we finished for the day and received our payment — three pails of potatoes — which to us was a small fortune!

Tired and happy, we returned with our wealth to the camp. The potato harvest was a blessing for us prisoners of war. Each one worked at his own pace to accumulate enough potatoes to tide him over. To avoid fights that might arise over the presence of so many potatoes in the barracks, Guenther Nagel kept them for us in the storage cellar of the kitchen. Our names were put on a list along with the number of potatoes per pail, and we were allowed to withdraw from our account at any time.

As far as I can remember, there was not one case of misconduct, or abuse of privileges reported to Natschalnik Movka throughout the entire potato harvest. When the harvest was over, he called us together one day, praising us, not only because we had kept his trust, but because we had not eased our efforts to deliver the norm!

Now that we could supplement the camp soup with our own food, we had more energy to devote to our work. This, combined with our improved skill at the stone quarry was the reason almost every track crew was able to achieve its norm, leaving before the end of the shift. We in track 3 were no exception. Like a bolt out of the blue, a "miracle tool" practically fell into our laps.

One day, I noticed an oversized rake among the other tools. It was a monster rake, with teeth ten inches long and a seven foot handle. No one else gave so much as a glance to this freak rake, but hoping to solve our sand and gravel problems, we adopted this orphan. Our efforts with this strange tool caused joking and pitying smiles from our comrades. Ludwig and I were often called "The Two Gardeners" — the name was very apt. We soon discovered that we not only saved time, but physical expenditure as well, by using this rake on our sand pile. Ludwig and I raked many lorries of gravel together, and soon the other tracks stopped smiling, and accepted us as serious competition.

The summer passed and the days grew shorter, while

the temperature fell noticeably. In the quarry, the drilling was stepped up, but there was no blasting. The holes were stuffed with wooden plugs, but for two days we were not allowed to go up the stone face to break stones. We were told all this was in preparation for one tremendous blast to loosen as many stones as possible before the snow and ice came. Shortly before the blasting, the quarry looked as if it had been swept clean. Our track number 3 was hardly recognizable; we had carted away twelve lorries of sand, and looked with pleasure at the stone wall!

The blast was a complete success and the entire camp hurried to the quarry to see the effects of the explosion. We could hardly believe our eyes at the prolfieration of stones. I doubt that an earthquake could have done a better job. Ludwig was so excited by our bonanza on track 3, he squeezed my arm, exclaiming.

"Knüppel! Santa Claus came early this year! Look at all the presents he's left us!"

The afternoon shift could hardly wait to get to the quarry, scoop up the stones, and leave early. At first everything went beautifully, then came the terrible news that the gravel mill had broken down and was being repaired. Waiting impatiently for the empty lorries, the prisoners angrily cursed worse than the Russians, but still the gravel mill remained silent. After about two and a half hours the mill was repaired, but there was no thought of returning to camp early.

Meanwhile, back in the camp, the first brigade received bad news from Guenther Nagel.

"Men," he began, "I have been informed by Movka that tomorrow is a collective work day, known popularly as "Stachonowski" Day. You all know the meaning of that! All of us will have to remain at the quarry for eight full hours, trying to achieve a 'supernorm'. During the day shift, the entire civilian staff connected with the quarry will work alongside us. Natschalnik Movka will personally supervise the whole operation."

A moment of stunned silence, then the storm broke

forcefully. The room was filled with furious discussion, and Nagel ordered silence. He continued,

"It's not Natschalnik Movka's fault, he's merely conveying orders from higher up. The only thing we can do is make the best of a bad bargain."

Brigadier Jellinek came to Nagel's aid,

"I agree with Guenther, men. Look at the situation from a practical point of view. Since we have no other alternative, let's play the game the way they want us to. I say we should get out there tomorrow and bury them in stones. In other words, we'll do a good job, and Movka will be praised for it, undoubtedly receiving a free stamp in his party book."

"And we get a kick in the ass!" Cousin threw out.

"Quite the contrary." Jellinek continued, "I think we will benefit it, too. Natschalnik Movka needs us as much as we need him. Remember how it was during the potato harvest? It's easier to do your work with a full stomach than an empty one!"

We argued this point for some time, and finally, wisdom prevailed over emotion.

Shortly before eight o'clock the next morning, Natschalnik Movka appeared, all business. He informed us that eight civilians were on the main track unloading the stones from the lorries. The rest of the civilians would work with us in the quarry.

Determinedly, our troop marched towards the quarry. Petrov, our good-natured guard, was told to put down his gun and take his place alongside us. His long rifle was replaced by an equally long crowbar. Proudly, with a decisive expression, he marched with us in the last row of the column.

Project "Stachnowski" was a complete success all the way down the line. Natschalnik Movka acted like a general on the battlefield, inspiring us. We worked in the quarry as if our lives depended on achieving super production. It is impossible to know how far a man can be pushed, before he finally collapses.

Guenther Nagel acted as a traffic policeman, too. His job was to direct the empty lorries to the different tracks, supervising the hauling of the full ones up the quarry incline. His alertness averted a serious accident — the lorries were coupled together and pulled up the steep incline by a heavy steel wire attached to a powerful winch. A line of lorries, loaded with their cargo, was almost at the top, when the last lorry became uncoupled, falling backwards with the speed of a locomotive, sparks flying from its screeching wheels. Suddenly, Nagel's commanding voice was heard,

"Take cover, men! Away from the track!"

Prisoners took off like scared rabbits as the lorry sped along the floor of the quarry, crashing into one standing on track number 7. Both were derailed with a deafening noise, spilling stones in all directions, but thanks to Nagel's presence of mind, not a single prisoner was injured.

At last the glorious "Stachonowski" Day was over, and Natschalnik Movka stood in the middle of the quarry, surrounded by his faithful helpers, announcing in a proud voice, the achievement of the supernorm.

Apparently no one had enough strength to yell "bravo" or "hurrah". We merely manifested a broad smile of accomplishment. But to me, the greatest achievement of that day was not the supernorm, but the rapport we developed with the Russians. On that day, we found ourselves promoted from prisoners to human beings. That, to my mind, was the real accomplishment!

On my birthday, November 30, 1947, the temperature slipped down to 40 degrees below zero. My brigade was scheduled for the second shift; six to three a.m. Until, now there were no indications that my birthday would be different from any other cold, miserable day. Yet, shortly before leaving for work that evening, I received my birthday surprise! It came whistling on wheels, an entire train to be loaded with stones!

In the summer months, stone loading was generally a welcome diversion from quarry work, but in the winter it was a gruesome ordeal, hated by everyone. Fulfilling the norm in winter took 8, 9 or even 10 hours. Sometimes we had to go in search of stones because there were not enough to load the train.

In addition, the stones were frozen together and covered with snow. Our gloves were cut to ribbons on the icy surfaces and it was impossible to warm our hands anywhere. We were constantly exposed to the merciless east wind, and, as bad as the day shift was, it was worse at night.

I knew how my comrades felt. Self-injury, escape, or dropping dead on the spot, seemed like a good solution! Anything to escape from this White Hell! I am not sure why I never took positive action, but this much is clear: to commit suicide or contrive a serious accident, takes more courage than most brave soldiers possess!

The Christmas Season came closer and the Yuletide Spirit was, in the truest sense of the word — lousy! Nothing but discontent, hunger and lice. There were more lice on our bodies, than hair on our heads. No mention was made of the coming holiday but I knew that each of us, thought of his loved ones. We had received no replies from our Red Cross postcards, and neither good omens, nor hope awaited our third Christmas in prison.

A few days before Christmas, rumors began circulating around the barracks. Prisoners who went many times a night to the latrine, insisted that Emil Muller was cooking in the kitchen late at night. Several men swore that they saw smoke coming from the chimney way after midnight.

Despite our spying and conjecturing, no information could be uncovered except that Emil must be up to something. Yet the little that we saw released all the wishful thoughts within us, and fantastic rumors were passed back and forth. We didn't suspect the truth would exceed our wildest imaginings!

On the evening of the twenty-third of December, some of us sat around a big table, peeling hot potatoes for the kitchen when Guenther Nagel entered.

"Listen everybody!" he said, "I have good news!"

Many expectant eyes looked up; and Nagel's voice had a happy ring to it, as he informed us,

"Men, tomorrow we won't have to work; we're going to celebrate Christmas Eve!"

Immediately a sound like the Indians' war whoop sounded simultaneously from several throats. Quieter types were smiling, surprised and grateful. Cousin let out a startled, "Well, kiss my ass!", and Ludwig was so surprised, he stuck a half-peeled potato into his gaping mouth.

Nagel tried desperately to quiet us, and we gave him our attention long enough to add,

"Wait! There's a catch! I was able to arrange it only after long negotiations with Natschalnik Movka. But we must make up for it by working the following Sunday. However, let's not spoil our Christmas Eve, tomorrow is ours!"

CHAPTER THIRTEEN

The anxiety and tension in the camp had reached the point where we were literally jumping with excitement. Around 6:00 p.m., we gathered around a primitive banquet table, waiting like children for the big surprise.

Finally, that moment came! The door was opened, and the kitchen volunteers entered with our dinner. It began with a thick, delicious soup, followed by the main course: potatoes, a slice of fried meat, and gravy. Pleasure beamed from every face. We had set up a makeshift Christmas tree, and after the feast, it looked good, after all.

When we had eaten, we lit cigarettes and sat around talking. Then, coming through the door, was surprise number two! Coffee and cake! We could scarcely believe our eyes. Each man received 12 pieces of cake, and some rich, aromatic coffee. The evening was made — anything more would be anti-climactic, we thought.

But after an hour or so, the third surprise arrived! In the door frame stood — Santa Claus!

As if he wanted to embrace us all, Santa Claus, or Guenther Nagel, raised his arms, jovially wishing us all Merry Christmas.

"My personal wish and prayer is that we should be in Germany with our loved ones next Christmas."

Speaking as one man, we spontaneously seconded the wish. Nagel was deeply touched, and continued,

"Sit down *Kameraden*. I've brought some surprises for each of you."

No words can describe our emotions as we received a package of tobacco, a loaf of bread, a half pound of sugar, and a big chunk of smoked salmon — my God, what a fortune!

Our eyes gazed on these sumptuous treasures with astonishment. We couldn't believe it was really true; but it was! Even Cousin and other characters who always had an answer for everything, were at a loss for words, they let their eyes do the talking.

Guenther Nagel and Emil Muller joined us at the table, beginning a night of good cheer and fellowship as we sang our favorite Christmas carols. We had just finished the third song, when Natschalnik Movka stuck his head in the door way. Nagel invited him to join us, but he declined our invitation at first. However, we encouraged him to share in our happiness. When Emil Muller brought him a cup of coffee and two pieces of cake, Natschalnik Movka rose, looked around with moist eyes, and said,

"Excuse me for intruding, but I didn't come to share your festivity or to spy on you. I was attracted by your singing, and I would like you to please continue as you were before I interrupted you."

As we continued singing, the Natschalnik sat and listened, thoughtfully.

For several hours, we forgot our surroundings and our present life. All credit for this unforgetable evening must go to Guenther Nagel and Emil Muller; their good will, selfless concern, and practicality had made it all possible. Nagel later explained how he had begun saving food from the time of the potato harvest.

The next day most of us were indisposed, but this blissful state of discomfort did not last long. Soon things returned to normal again, and our life took its usual course.

New Year's Day lay behind us, and the year 1948 entered in the worst possible way — ice, snow, blizzards and very low temperatures. The first two months should have been removed from the calendar. The White Hell slashed at us with its fierce claws, and those grim companions, the cold and the icy east wind, paralyzed us. The work progress and our physical condition reached an alltime low.

There were terrible cases of frost bite, and anyone who could get himself written up as a bed case was a man to be envied. This situation continued throughout February.

One day around the end of the month, Natschalnik Movka entered the barracks, asking if there were two prisoners who wanted some extra work. Ludwig and I jumped at the opportunity and before the camp gate we were given over to a civilian, who left with us.

While we stomped through the snow, I spoke to our employer. The good man's name was Sascha, and he worked as a railroad engineer. He said he wanted us to cut some wood for him. After walking approximately two miles we reached his house. In front was a mountain of railway ties. Ludwig had a cynical look in his eyes, as Sascha suggested,

"Let's go inside. I'll give you a saw."

I sensed trouble when I looked at the crude two man saw which must have been as old as the Urals. Sascha told us how long he wanted the pieces cut, and with an encouraging *Dawai!* hustled us out the door.

My forebodings were justified when the saw caught and buckled; it was so dull, I doubt it could have sliced cheese. The pebbles and tar on the ice-covered ties became the final adversary. Ludwig regarded the pile of ties despairingly, a groan escaping his throat. We jerked the saw handles frantically, our faces turning purple from frost and anger. Occasionally, we looked at each other accusingly. Before Ludwig and I became bitter enemies, we ceased the ludicrous undertaking and stormed into the house.

What a waste of energy! Without mincing words, I told Sascha we could not do the job with that miserable saw! Sascha looked at it, nodded in agreement and said,

"One day I'll buy myself another one."

The only good part of the whole undertaking was that Sascha never returned for us to finish the job!

Slowly but surely, the rigors of winter declined; soon it was the 23rd of March, 1948. Three full years of prison life had passed, and even the stones in the quarry started whispering about it. From every sign, the quarry was awakening from the long winter's sleep. As the warm sun beams melted the ice, the Russian workers said, superstitiously, "Listen! The stones are talking."

Finally, the entire land became free of ice, and the retreat of "General Winter" was only a matter of days. Flocks of birds brought the joyful news of the ensuing celebration. The message was heard by all men, animals, and even prisoners of war.

We could work more productively in the quarry now, but there were new dangers, too. Suddenly and without warning, large masses of stones would break away from the grip of the ice and thunder downwards. Miraculously, no one was injured.

Beguiled by the richness of stone in the quarry, I laid aside my caution frequently coming within a hair's breadth of death. One day while working frenetically around a keystone, which could bring an entire wall of stone tumbling down if loosened, Ludwig shouted a warning. I reacted with lightning speed, and for several seconds, death breathed down my neck, as an avalanche of stones rained down. In a state of shock, I climbed down to the bottom of the quarry where I was given a soothing cigarette. Then Ludwig asked me with an ironic grin,

"What's the matter; you tired of living?"

"You call this life?" I answered feebly. I was in no mood for humor, now!

The spring medical examination which all the prisoners had been awaiting hopefully, was a great disappointment. All those declared unfit by the Novotnik were either poor workers or troublemakers. We suspected collusion in her decisions, but couldn't protest. Yet this much was true beyond a doubt, we would remain behind even though we were already as thin as broom handles.

It was time again for May Day, and the *Natschalnik* made a speech giving us the rest of the day off. This contrasted with the free workers of Tscheljabinsk, who had to participate in marches and demonstrations until late at night.

The norm machine continued to grind without let-up, and once more the intense competition between crews and brigades was accelerated. We were now allowed to accept outside work again, willingly taking whatever opportunities we could find.

Ludwig and I did very well, finding work that was not only well paying, but interesting. We helped redecorate the house of a "Kirghiz" family. The homeland of the brave and proud Kirghiz people is in Central Asia, and our employer belonged to a tribe famed for its horsemanship, known as the Kara-Kirgizen (the Black Caps). The most formal room in the house was decorated in their traditional style, having a touch of Oriental splendor. It might have come right out of the Arabian Nights. On the floor, standing in the centre of a thick Persian rug, was a highly polished samovar.

In Ludwig's opinion, all this exotic beauty paled before the charm of the eighteen year old Reika, the pride of the family. He would rave for hours about this "Beauty of Beauties", calling her the wild flower of the Orient, the priceless gem from the East, and all the other flowery phrases he knew.

After one visit, when Ludwig began to praise Reika in poetic terms, I stopped suddenly, put my hand on his forehead, and said,

"Tell me, Omar, are you really in love, or are you just plain sick?"

He threw me a devastating look, and strode away without uttering another word, ignoring me for the rest of the day.

Was it an accident, or was it fate? Ludwig slipped and fell from the stone wall where he was busy breaking stone. He was reported as sick, but fortunately, the accident was not serious. Thank goodness, all he endured were some small bruises and skin lacerations. I went several times by myself to the Kirghiz family to finish our work. They showed concern for Ludwig, and wished him a speedy recovery. When the work was finished, we were well paid in produce. I carried back to the camp a pail of potatoes, a loaf of bread, and some fresh vegetables. In addition, we were given forty rubles.

We exchanged our "Dozwidania's" and I was ready to leave. Reika saw me to the door; there, she sneaked me two packages of Machorka.

"Send Ludwig my best wishes," she said in her melodious voice, giving me a smile that would melt all the ice in Siberia. Her eyes shone like emeralds and it was easy for me to see what Ludwig felt for her.

In search of more work, I came to an old, isolated house. I was going to ignore it, but for some unknown reason, I changed my mind and knocked on the door. From within, a voice shouted: "Come on in!" I opened the door, entering the darkened interior of a typical Russian peasant's house. An old man was sitting at the table, slurping soup. Without rising, he looked me over asking finally,

"Are you hungry?"

"Yes." I answered.

"Come and sit down."

Bewildered at the prospect of obtaining a meal so easily, I sat down opposite him. While I ate my bread and soup, we observed one another. The man had small pig eyes, the wisdom of Mother Russia emanating from them. In the centre of his face was a nose like a frost-bitten potato, while his bushy white beard grew in all directions like wild underbrush.

When I could no longer bring the spoon to my mouth because I was filled to the gills, I smiled gratefully at my host. But before I could say a word of thanks, he asked,

"You're a prisoner of war, aren't you?"

"Yes."

"Are you escaping?"

"On the contrary. I'm looking for extra work to fill my stomach better."

The man smiled, appearing relieved. As we rolled ourselves cigarettes from his tobacco, he declared,

"My name is Grisha. What's yours?"

"Kurt."

"German?'

I nodded my assent.

"Where do you work, Kurt?"

"In the stone quarry."

Grisha leaned back, letting out a long whistle through his tobacco stained teeth.

We continued smoking silently for a while, then he leaned over to me, saying,

"You know, Kurt, not far from here there are a lot of Volga German women." He winked slyly, "You should visit them as soon as you can; you'll find it worth your while, I'm sure!"

Then he described the location, giving me instructions to get there. I thanked my host, resolving to take his advice at the earliest possible moment.

Unfortunately, Ludwig could not leave the camp the next Sunday, so I went to visit the girls myself. Guenther Nagel gave me permission to go, and Petrov told me to watch out for the police. The weather was simply beautiful as I walked across open fields. It was a long hike, but very pleasant.

Finally, I saw the women's barracks, exactly as described by Grisha. I walked timidly to the nearest one.

On the porch, I introduced myself in German to a young woman who returned my greeting in a friendly manner; then everything went along beautifully. Before I knew it, I was inside the building, and the cynosure of many female eyes. In a moment, I was besieged by questions on all sides. Lena, a young, good looking woman came to my aid, saying,

"You must be hungry after all that walking. I'll get you something to eat."

I couldn't believe my eyes. Before me was set a dish of pancakes, and next to it a glass full of milk. Apparently no one wanted to be left out, and the women stacked bread on each side of the table. With delight, my eyes wandered over the mounting pile of fresh-smelling bread.

Finally, I was satiated. Even with good intentions, I couldn't swallow another mouthful. As the cigarette burned, I felt an indescribable sense of contentment, and I must confess that I really enjoyed being the centre of attention. I learned that there were 150 Volga German women living in three barracks. They performed compulsory work in a nearby factory. Some of them were married, but their husbands worked elsewhere, also in forced labor for the development of Russia.

I showed them my gratitude by entertaining them with monologues from my repertoire. I began by reciting witty stories, and greatly inspired by so many females, my talent became hypnotic as I charmed this completely responsive audience. The sense of timing I had acquired told me when to bring my performance to a close, and as a finale, I did my infamous "Woman Undressing" scene. It could not have been better chosen. The applause, the surprised faces, the ingenuous laughter of my audience told me I had really scored a hit!

As I was saying good-bye, and stuffing the bread into my rucksack, several women came over, shook my hand, and discreetly left a ruble note in my palm.

Lena showed me to the door, saying,

"Come back soon. The women in the other barracks would love to see you too!"

Drawn together by mutual attraction, our eyes sought one another in silent yearning. No words were spoken, they would only have broken the spell. Lena's eyes invited me with a frankness that was unmistakably obvious. For a short time, I felt like a man again, an emotion that the long prison confinement had completely erased. It was an enchanted atmosphere for us; one that would grow with each visit.

In the summer of 1948, almost all of us in the quarry had a small business on the side. Our camp barber had a steady clientele among the Russians, and there were two comrades who were watch-makers by trade. Others made brass rings and engravings, all highly polished, and still others whittled small masterpieces, figurines, picture frames, and even mousetraps.

Ludwig and I did not go hungry either; we worked as middle-men for the camp artisans. There were 150 German "Sisters" whom we visited, selling them many of the items made in the camp, deducting a small percentage for ourselves.

Watches and clocks of all shapes and sizes were taken back to the camp to be repaired. Our business flourished, but not without anxiety. Ludwig and I were in constant fear our gold mine would be discovered by the others.

Occasionally, we dropped by to visit the Kirghiz

family. They did not have any more work for us, but they always gave us a friendly greeting and something to eat. As we sat around the table, Reika and Ludwig openly flirted. I thought they were too obvious and too bold, and the next time we dropped in, Reika was not present. Her father said she was visiting relatives.

Another time, only her mother was present. From the cool reception we received, one could surmise our visits were not welcome anymore. Ludwig, like most people in love was riding on pink clouds.

On the way back to the camp, we had a heated debate. At first I tried to help him by appealing to reason. Humorously, I recited,

" 'If someone climbs a tree, it doesn't mean he's a bird'."

"Ludwig looked at me, surprised and angry. He turned on his heel and marched away, and it was some time before I caught up with him. We walked together in silence because Ludwig was angry. Suddenly he asked, suspiciously,

"Tell me, Professor, what gives you the right to butt into my private business?"

"Look who's talking. You put your nose into mine recently, if I remember correctly!"

"Just what do you mean by that?"

"Do you remember back in the main camp, when I stood with one foot in the boat and one on the shore?"

"So!?"

"Well — didn't you try to soothe my tormented soul by giving me friendly advice?"

"I guess so." he conceded, reluctantly.

"Well, as your friend, I'm returning the favor, trying to keep you from being hurt!"

"Knüppel, for crying out loud, I don't know what the hell you're talking about!"

"Then let me explain, Ludwig! You're as blind as a bat when it comes to Reika! Not that I don't like her, on the contrary, she's a lovely girl. But let's face facts, she's meant for someone else, and her parents are trying in a polite way to enlighten you."

"Do you mean they're trying to put a stop to things?"

" 'Out of sight, out of mind' !" I exclaimed.

"Do you really think they sent her away so we couldn't see each other?"

"Ludwig, wake up! Reika wasn't away at all! She was in the upstairs room."

He looked at me, bewildered,

"Just now, as we left, I looked back and saw Reika's face in the window."

"Are you sure?" he groaned.

"Positive, Ludwig", I continued. "Try to forget her, because it's senseless to keep returning there. Her parents object to it very strenuously."

"They haven't said a thing to me." Ludwig said, stubbornly.

"Why should they? Besides your financial and social situation is hardly worth discussing."

Too late, I realized that I had said too much. Ludwig gave me a long, agonized look and without saying anything he stood up slowly and looked despairingly towards Reika's house. Then the turned around and stomped away; the name Reika was never mentioned between us again.

The summer of 1948 came to an end and there was a rumor that mail was on the way. Then one day the unbelievable happened — the mail arrived! Finally we held a message in our trembling hands, a sign of love from our dears ones.

Several comrades shook their Red Cross postcards in their outstretched hands, weaving it as if it were the prison release. Everywhere were smiling faces and moist eyes.

Cousin could not restrain his joy, but proclaimed loudly to no one in particular,

"Well, kiss my ass! What do you know!? One of my brothers is home already! And get a load of this! He tells me he has a stand on the market and needs my help desperately. I'd better hurry and pack!"

I read the postcard from my mother over and over again. My heart overflowed with thankfulness and joy; God be thanked, my parents were well, and living as well as could be expected. From my wife — not one syllable. As much as I racked my brains, I could find no satisfying explanation for her neglect. There were hundreds of possibilities, all of which started with a "maybe".

My friend Ludwig received good news from home.

Several comrades, however, were unlucky because they received no messages. Disappointed and bitter, they stole away from our temple of joy and sat dejected and alone.

The news from home released a wealth of new rumors which were not different from the old ones, except that we used brighter colors to paint pictures of the home transports. Our wishful thoughts created masterpieces, but unfortunately, the year was indecipherable as it was written in small print on the bottom of the picture.

The potato harvest came around again and was greeted joyfully and expectantly. We were as busy as beavers and thrifty as squirrels for the coming winter. Each one tried to exceed his previous potato surplus, and good organization, a better knowledge of quarry work, and particularly the rapport with the Russian civilians made it possible for us to reach high goals.

It was a good harvest and profitable for all, while the great fall blasting operation signalled the end of summer. "Stachonowski Day" was announced, and this, as it turned out, was to be our farewell to the stone quarry!

The following day, we were ordered to stand in formation.

"Men!" Movka began, "Yesterday we proved again that we are able to surpass our norm. We almost doubled the daily output from the quarry, and I am very pleased and proud of our achievement."

The Natschalnik looked at his boots, searching for the inspiration to continue. Looking up again, his eyes wandered over our ranks.

"This morning I received an order from my superior, saying that you will be returned to the main camp in Tscheljabinsk this coming Sunday, I wasn't told the reason, but whatever it may ve, I would like to add that because of working together for many months, I have learned much about you people. I'm very unhappy to lose you, as workers as well as comrades. That's all. *Doxwidania.*" (Good-bye).

We were dismissed, and in the barracks a storm broke loose. Hands were shaken, as cries of happiness, questions and speculations issued forth. We chattered like magpies — however, one thought kept reiterating, "We're going home!"

Guenther Nagel entered the room and the chatter stopped immediately. In the hushed silence, our questioning eyes avidly watched his lips.

"If you guys think I know any more than you, you're wrong. I am as confused as you are. Certainly there's been a lot of talk in the camp about home transports, but that's a part of our daily lfie and nothing new. I suggest that we hope for the best, and be prepared for the worst."

Ludwig felt the order should have come three months earlier if we were going home. However, on the doorstep of winter, it seemed practical to return to the main camp.

Slowly, we calmed down, trying to adjust to the new situation. We were very much concerned about our stored up food supplies, so we simply commenced feasting, even though Christmas was months away. Until Sunday, we lived like the worm in the bacon, gorging urselves and celebrating. Yes indeed, we said good-bye in fine style. I can say everyone, without exception, was happy to leave his bone-breaking work. "Breaking Stones in Siberia", was a proverbial statement, which I had heard often. But few people realize the true meaning of it, unless they have seen the rivers of blood and sweat with their own eyes.

The first days back in the main camp were filled with the usual formalities. We remained in two brigades, one under Jellinek, and the other under Guenther Nagel; also Emil Muller was reassigned to the kitchen as cook.

We were named the "All Purpose" Brigades, because we did every menial job conceivable, work which made it difficult to attain the norm, including such tasks as snow shovelling, piling iron, construction work, unloading coal, and so forth. Yet miraculously, every night when we returned to the barracks, we still had 600 grams of bread to eat. The persuasive powers of Guenther Nagel and Jellinek who had pressured the supervisors for our nariats, were to be thanked for it. As usual, there were plenty of rumors about going-home-transport, but there was no indication who the lucky ones would be.

The new barracks, including metal beds, and luxurious straw sacks could not compensate for the loss of small advantages we had enjoyed so much in the quarry. The wind in Camp 6/10 blew from a different direction and we had to adjust fast!

Once more the slogan was "I, me and myself". Jellinek and Nagel tried hard to keep us together, but slowly, under the rigorous daily struggle, we drifted apart. I considered myself fortunate in having two good buddies like Peter and Ludwig; friendships like that were priceless.

As a special favor, the quarry brigades were invited to attend the opening night of the culture group. It was good to say hello to a few old timers, but there were many new faces, too. Also, the culture group had a surplus of talents.

Rohdenbach and Wetzlaff greeted us with an artificial friendliness, and Rohdenbach asked if we were interested in acting in the Christmas Program. Ludwig and I were hesitant, but finally Ludwig said,

"I don't know, August. I'm all packed and ready to go home. I'll let you know."

And I added, "That goes for me too, August."

The performance made a tremendous impression on me because the production was of a professional calibre. No improvisation, no second hand stuff, but showmanship in its fullest at sense. Later. I asked Ludwig, why he had been so sarcastic.

"Because of their attitude! I don't like the way they offered us the crumbs." He hit me on the shoulder, adding, "I'm not going to crawl back to them, licking their boots! They can keep it, those ignorant bastards!"

I tried to calm him, but he just shouted,

"What's the matter. Do you have cotton in your ears? I can still hear Wetzlaff's slimy voice, 'Well now! How are our hard working quarry workers today?' That did it!"

In a way he was right. I just had to let him get the steam out of his system. I knew my friend too well, he was the kind of guy who let everything build up inside, then blew up all at once. Secretly, I felt his problem was not really Rohdenbach and Wetzlaff.

November 30, 1948, my twenty-eight birthday. As a birthday present I received a cold turkey — picking ice and shovelling snow on the railroad tracks. The time passed so slowly, it seemed an eternity. In this cold weather, probably even all the clocks had frozen, but eventually, the order came for us to turn in our tools. It sounded like a Beethoven symphony to me.

Marching back to the camp, I noticed something was wrong with Ludwig. He stumbled along, and a few times nearly fell to the ground. I asked,

"What's the matter?"

He said, "Boy, am I beat! I feel so tired, I can hardly lift my feet."

After we reached the barracks, I had a close look at him. There was no doubt about it, he had fever. His forehead was hot and his eyes confirmed it. Besides he coughed in short, dry spasms that worried me.

I made him go to sick bay where it was discovered he had a temperature of 104 degrees. He was admitted to the hospital immediately. What a birthday I had! Depressed, hungry, and worried about my friend, I lay in my bunk, staring up into emptiness. I remembered the chocolate cake mother had baked for me every year until my 19th birthday and I had been away from home for the last nine. With my remaining strength, I mentally, blew out twenty-eight candles.

The next day, right after work, I hurried to the hospital where Ludwig was asleep. I asked Dr. Meinicke about his condition. He said he wasn't sure yet — what most concerned him was the high fever. After a week the fever broke, but Ludwig was practically a skeleton, sleeping almost all day and night. Thank God, it was not pneumonia.

In the camp Christmas rumors were thick. Of course, some appeared in the most imaginative Christmas trimmings.

But the unbelievable finally happened! A transport was put together quickly. Since the names of the lucky ones had not yet been released, an atmosphere of supressed excitement hung over the camp. Preparations for the transport went on constantly. Finally, on December 8th the names of the lucky ones were released. Besides the usual sick list, there were quite a number of healthy, ablebodied prisoners. Mouse, our little friend from Dresden, was among them. It was high time, he had shrivelled to a mere ninety pounds. Peter and I were not on the list, of course, but our dear friend Ludwig was!

It is hard for me to describe my feelings. Naturally, I was overjoyed that he was going home. Yet I could not bear the thought of losing him. The word 'friend" can be found in any dictionary or crossword puzzle but it has been used and abused so that it has lost meaning. Ludwig was an important part of my life and close to my heart.

At the hospital, I sat on his bed trying to think of something sensible to say. Finally, I remarked,

"By the way things are developing, they really mean it this time."

"Yes", he agreed, "From what I hear, they're going to start loading the train in a few days."

"Listen, buddy, if everything goes well, you'll be home by Christmas Eve. Just make sure, you be there on time!"

Ludwig's response was quite unexpected. His feverish eyes filled with anxiety and he pulled the thermometer from under his arm-pit, handing it to me without a word. Looking away, he asked hoarsely.

"How much?"

I did not trust my eyes; the mercury registered 104 degrees.

"How high is it?" he gasped.

Tonelessly, I answered, "104."

"This morning it was only 100." Ludwig groaned.

Before I left the hospital, I conferred with Dr. Meinicke. He said Ludwig undoubtedly had suffered a relapse. Poor Ludwig continued to worsen, and his name was finally taken off the going-home list.

It was hard for him to get over this disappointment. Mentally and physically, hope became dim. He no longer put up the old fight for life. Peter and I did our utmost to reawaken Ludwig's will to survive, even trying Kinderman's medicine. Dr. Meinicke explained that he should be grateful he did not leave with the transport, because he wouldn't have survived the trip.

I will skip Christmas, 1948; for us, it was no Christmas at all. The way I felt, I could have slept through the whole season, from Christmas to New Year's!

Early in January, the quarry brigades were dissolved, and I was told that I was returning to Schitz. This delighted me so, I felt like jumping in the air for joy; but lacking the energy, I merely sat down and rolled myself a cigarette.

I had a feeling Peter must have had something to do with my good luck. When I saw him next, I asked him directly,

"How did you manage it?"

He answered me mischievously, "Never mind. I'm

not fond of visits to the hospital; one sick friend is quite enough for me."

Later when I told Ludwig the happy news, I was glad to see him taking an interest again. Very much relieved; I left the hospital.

Returning to Schitz was like homecoming. Although I was no longer a brigadier, I still worked for Alexei. I was touched by the friendliness of my fellow workers when they welcomed me back. I wanted to say hello to Kostja — but first I had to find him.

After looking in several places, I discovered his new sleeping quarters. He greeted me with a big yawn, said how happy he was to see me, and with a 'See you later' curled up like a cat in dreamland.

Meeting Luba again was like inhaling a breath of spring air. She was most voluptuous, but being a prisoner of war more than dissipates one's amorous ideas, and limits one's appetites to the stomach. So I could enjoy my dreams while greeting her with a friendly hello, that she returned with a dazzling smile.

January, with all its terror, and depression passed. Early in February a new order was issued, raising our hopes tremendously. We were allowed to let our hair grow. The 'experts' analysed this as the best sign yet for going-home-transports. Combs were mass produced, and the carpenters became busy manufacturing wooden suitcases. Many prisoners were now receiving a small portion of the money they earned at the factory. 'Salaries' ranged from 20 to 150 rubles a month, and since the ruble was more stable at this point, even these small sums affected camp life. Those who were rich enough to afford the extra food, gave their soup and kascha to the poor devils in exchange for little services.

As our hair grew, the barbers began to give some individuality to our hair, and our faces developed character, even showing intelligence!

February dragged on; but it was mercifully short. In March, the sun tried bravely to melt the snow; but the nights were bitter cold. On March 10th, as I returned from work, without expecting anything in particular, Peter ran excitedly over and grabbed my arm, saying,

"Kurt! I must tell you something right away!"

"What's up, Peter?"

"Don't say anything; just follow me."

We entered my barracks where Peter almost pushed me into my bunk, then sat down next to me. Lowering his voice, he said,

"Listen carefully, Kurt! In a few days a transport will be put together, and you and Ludwig are going to be on THAT transport! What do you say to that?!"

The blood hammered against my temples, and I could not speak from excitement. Unconsciously, I grabbed my tobacco and began rolling a cigarette with shaking hands. Peter's face told me he was serious, but I still couldn't believe it. Finally I asked,

"What about you, Peter?"

"Not this time, Kurt" He excused himself saying, "Have to go now, be back as soon as I can."

To quell my excitement, I walked around the camp, seeking different places where I might find out more information. However, I knew more than anyone. Finally, I went to the hospital to see Ludwig, but I was not allowed in, because a medical examination was going on. Half frozen, I walked back to the barracks to warm myself. I was so restless, I could scarcely contain myself. Hours later I lay on my bunk, looked at the ceiling while doubts assailed me. It must have been around 9 o'clock when the door suddenly opened, and Peter walked in. From a list he read several names.

"Hurry up, you guys! You're going home! Schwefel is waiting for you at the administration barracks."

Not a soul moved for a second, but then all hell broke loose! The lucky ones, including myself, danced with frenzied steps. We were half mad with happiness and made no attempt to hide it.

Outside the administration building, I joined a long line of prisoners. We stood there with chattering teeth in the 42 below zero temperature, frozen stiff as boards, but didn't dare to leave our place because we might be called.

At around 11 o'clock, Schwefel came out, ordering, "Return to your barracks, and come back again at 8 o'clock tomorrow morning."

The news of the home transport was already common knowledge in camp. We learned that there would be seventy-five able-bodied prisoners, besides the sick ones. The rest of the transport would consist of men from the surrounding camp in Tscheljabinsk.

Sleep that night was out of the question, and next morning, we stood waiting before the door of the administration building. It was a strange feeling now to watch the work brigades passing through the gate. Slowly, it dawned on me that I really was not dreaming — everything seemed to be real!

When it was my turn to enter the 'Holy Rooms' of the G.P.U., a feeling of uneasiness came over me. I feared that something would go wrong. I saluted, removed my fur cap, and waited for what would come. The G.P.U. Chief looked at me penetratingly, but before he could speak Lieutenant Schwefel told him all he knew about me. His picture was correct, and I must say, impressive. The G.P.U. Chief read my dossier, appearing to be satisfied. Finally, he said, "*Chroroscho*, Stock — Go home!"

I was dismissed.

After that everything moved quickly. We received our transport clothing which was clean, and ninety percent new. Several of the camp nobility were on the transport, too — Rohdenbach, Heini Kuhnert, Traber-Karl, Konrad Kohlmeyer, Guenther Nagel, and the hammer leader from the Devil's Brigade. By now, I was sure that Ludwig would be with the sick, but I did not have a chance to talk to him during the preparations.

The joyful atmosphere was very hard to describe. For example, while we were washing, we laughed and threw water at one another. Words were heard which no one had spoken for years. Peter came to say good-bye, and we spoke meaningless, empty phrases which conveyed little of what we felt. What words could convey four years of human degradation, and a friendship that had outlasted all of it? There were no words in any language to communicate our emotions.

I tried to cheer Peter, but he interrupted me before I could say anything.

"Do you know what Lieutenant Schwefel told me today, Kurt?"

"What?"

"Schwefel promised I would be on the next transport going home!"

I looked questioningly into Peter's face, feeling that he wanted to make it easy for us. Then again, he might have been telling the truth.

CHAPTER FOURTEEN

The 13th of March, 1949! "Attention!" someone shouted, as Lieutenant Schwefel entered the room followed by two other officers.

"At ease, men," he ordered. Then he made a short farewell speech,

"You are not allowed to take any written material along with you on the transport. This is your last chance to get rid of diaries, lists of addresses, and so forth. Leave them on the table in front of you. I must warn you, that if anything is found on you during the transport, there will be serious consequences."

Then he went casually through our belongings.

After the Russians left, we were sealed off from the rest of the prisoners. We sat around impatiently, waiting like men on top of a hot stove.

Finally, the order was given to assemble before the camp gate. Our names were called, and as each was called, he went through the gate, falling into formation on the other side. As the group became smaller and smaller, and still my name was not called, panic mounted within me. Finally, I heard it, and I dashed forward so quickly, I nearly trampled the Russian officer.

After four years, my deepest wish had come true, and I read the inscription. "He who does not work, shall not eat!" for the last time.

While we marched to the station, the trucks bearing the sick passed us. There must be something to Ludwig's superstitiousness, I thought. The number 13 was lucky for him. When we got to the station, we were immediately loaded into the boxcars. It was bitter cold, and in the centre of each car stood a stove, around which a considerable amount of wood was stacked. It did not take us long to start the stove, and in no time it was blazing hot; but still the train did not move.

After endless hours, the door was opened. Outside stood one officer and two guards who called a prisoner's name. He was told to pick up his things and follow them. He didn't return, and I never found out what happened to him.

Soon afterwards, the train started rocking back and forth, and a prisoner lost his balance falling against the red hot stove, and piercing the air with heart-rending screams.

He was taken off the train and transferred to the hospital. At last, we were on our way, but though the stove was blazing, the temperature inside the box-car was below zero, and the only warm spot was next to the stove. We took turns warming ourselves around it, and no one slept that night. What did it matter? The important thing was that we were moving West!

During the night, we crossed the Ural mountains. Our

first stop was Ufa. Here we received provisions: hot soup, bread, hot coffee, and a small amount of sugar. We were advised to gather as much wood as we could. To our surprise, we noticed that the doors were not locked any more, and our transport guards were pleasant, calling us "Comrade", and treating us like human beings.

We walked around, stretched our legs, and relieved our bladders; there were neither guns, or orders to walk in a circle. Everything contributed to our happiness. The train pushed on steadily, and by nightfall we reached Kubysov. It was obvious by now that we were returning along the same route we had come. The train reached Saransk early the next morning where there was a long stop-over. Food was distributed and wood gathered as before.

I attempted to seek out Ludwig, finding him standing before his boxcar. I was some distance away, and shouted his name as loud as I could. He looked around, noticing me. Overjoyed, he opened his arms, blurting out," "Hey there, Knüppelowski — let me embrace you, my son!"

I ran over to him and we acted like children at a reunion. He showed me his boxcar, and I stayed with him until the engine gave the warning signal to get ready.

Soon, we were on our way again. The sun broke the cold around noon, and we caught up on the sleep we had lost the night before. One small stop, then we pushed onward, to the Moscow suburbs.

There I had the opportunity to visit Ludwig again; we travelled together in his boxcar to Smolensk, talking the whole way, and smoking like chimneys.

In Smolensk, we received another surprise. Four boxcars were added, transporting 200 German women, also going home. Later we spoke to them, learning they had been in prison camps, just like ourselves. Their ages varied from twenty to forty; some carried babies with them as souvenirs of Russia. Many of them had left Germany as young healthy girls, and returned sick and prematurely aged.

A Russian guard standing nearby said to me, "Why don't you visit them? The trip is long and you'll probably have a lot to talk about," he winked encouragingly.

The train whistle put an end to this suggestion, but I promised to visit them at the next stop. For a while, the main topic of conversation was about girls, and everything concerning them. Undoubtedly, the first steps toward a normal life were made right here. No more talk about norms, fish soup, the cold, the wet bread, snow shovelling, or lice! Rohdenbach seemed to be particularly inspired by the opposite sex; it was as if a spring inside him was released suddenly. He entertained us with his stage anecdotes and intimate stories of situations behind the theatre curtains.

Some people like Rohdenbach have a gift for telling stories, but he made himself unpopular by switching to politics. Apparently he intended to continue brain-washing us all the way to Germany.

Traber-Karl saved us by changing the subject to the race tracks and, of course, his amorous adventures with the high class ladies.

As for myself, I was saturated with their clap-trap and I could hardly wait for the next stop to scramble out to see Ludwig again.

An incident occurred at this stop which I must mention — a group of prisoners were sent to fetch water for the transport kitchen, and accidentally, two were left behind. This was immediately reported to the officer at the next stop. His concern and quick action amazed us; he ordered the engine uncoupled from the train and sent back for the two prisoners. As the engine pulled into the station with the two men aboard, the air was filled with our triumphant shouting.

The next stop was Minsk where Ludwig and I took advantage of the invitation extended by the girls to join them. Our hostesses were as friendly as could be, apologizing that they could serve us nothing. A girl of about twenty-five introduced herself as Margaret Koenig from Leipzig. As Margaret told me, their situation as prisoners of war had been similar to ours; but they suffered from another disadvantage as well. Being females, they were the prey of every male in the vicinity. They were bribed with food, seduced, and in a few cases, even raped. This explained the few babies they carried with them. The girls had been guarded very closely, but somehow the kitchen staff and other men managed to find their way to the girls' quarters.

When we arrived at the border city of Brest, the four cars with the girls were uncoupled and put on another track. We were ordered to leave our cars and fall into line. The station guards and soldiers were different from those who accompanied us on the transport. They pushed us along, cursing and spitting, and we were counted and recounted. Our uwillingness to cooperate annoyed them, and we even received a threat from the officer in charge that he would send the whole transport back if we did not conform at once.

That convinced us, and soon we were led to a barracks area and given food. After we had eaten, our belongings and even our clothing were taken from us and thoroughly searched, Our clothes were deloused and we had to submit to an even tougher cleaning procedure.

Each prisoner was cross-examined by interrogation experts, and when my turn came, I was marched inside a circle drawn on the floor. Two officers sat on the table, staring at me, while a Russian Sergeant investigated every inch of my body, looking for scars and tattoo marks and who knows what else. Questions were thrown at me, such as, "Were you in the S.S.?" — "Which unit did you belong to?" — "Where did you serve during the war?" and so forth. They did their utmost, looking for something that would send me back. The examination dragged on interminably, but finally the ordeal ended.

As far as I know, they found three men guilty, and put them in the brig. I don't know what happened to them later. On one, a scar was discovered which they claimed was formerly the S.S. tattoo. Another, stepped into a trap when he admitted belonging to a unit which was apparently on the Russian's black list, and the third hid a diary in the false bottom of his suitcase. As Ludwig told me later, they had not been too particular with the sick prisoners. Finally, we were led to the boxcars again and the transport started moving, entering the two mile stretch of "no man's land" between Poland and Russia, which consisted of two miles of barbed wire, mine fields, pill boxes, heavy guards and machine guns.

In our boxcar everyone was awed; even Rohdenbach and Traber Karl kept their mouths shut, feeling the significance of the moment. There were no jokes, no hurrahs, but it seemed everyone was silently praying.

As we entered Polish territory, we were indescribably happy to leave Russia behind. We travelled with open doors, singing and laughing ecstatically. As soon as we left Warsaw, it was only a matter of time before we crossed the German border, and with every kilometer, our excitement became harder to control. Finally, when the train passed the Oder Bridge, we reached the summit of happiness. The sun shone brightly in the blue sky, on that memorable March 29th, 1949, as the train pulled into Frankfurt on der Oder. A band was playing while civilians stood about silently following the train with their eyes, searching for a loved one, a friend, or a husband.

Don't give up looking and don't give up hope! Mothers, fathers, wives! We are not the last ones. Many more unsung heros of the Rehabilitation Brigades are still back there!

May the Lord protect and guide them safely home.

BOOK BARGAINS — FOR ONLY $1.25

IF UNAVAILABLE AT YOUR BOOKSTORE OR NEWSSTAND MAIL THIS COUPON

Mail Service Department, **SIMON & SCHUSTER OF CANADA LTD.,**
225 Yonge Street North, Richmond Hill, Ontario, Canada.

Please send me the following book bargains:

NO. OF COPIES	AMT.	IBM #	TITLE	PRICE
....	....	78184	THE DEATH OF THE TORONTO TELE-GRAM AND OTHER NEWSPAPER STORIES — Jock Carroll. The death throes of a great newspaper and other round-the-world adventures.	$1.25
....	....	78078	WILD GOOSE JACK — Jack Miner. The autobiography of one of Canada's first great conservationists and bird lovers.	$1.25
....	....	78085	NO MANDATE BUT TERROR — G. Radwanski and K. Windeyer. An in-depth study of the revolutionary move-ment in Quebec.	$1.25
....	....	78025	MEMOIRS OF A BIRD IN A GILDED CAGE — Judy LaMarsh. A frank and witty account of back-room political battles by Canada's most controversial woman politician.	$1.25
....	....	78091	BRIGHT WORLD AROUND US — Miller and Margaret Stewart. True stories about wildlife, bears, moose, wolves, birds, cougars, squirrels and raccoons.	$1.25
....	....	78181	FACE-OFF — Scott Young and George Robertson. The love affair of a hockey star and a rock singer — which was made into an exciting motion picture.	$1.25

TOTAL AMOUNT ....

PLUS 25¢ HANDLING CHARGE

TOTAL ENCLOSED .... PLEASE SEND CHEQUE OR MONEY ORDER. WE ARE NOT RESPONSIBLE FOR ORDERS CONTAIN-ING CASH.

NAME ....

ADDRESS ....

CITY .... PROVINCE ....

HOCKEY BOOK BARGAINS

IF UNAVAILABLE AT YOUR BOOKSTORE OR NEWSSTAND MAIL THIS COUPON

Mail Service Department, **SIMON & SCHUSTER OF CANADA LTD.,**
225 Yonge Street North, Richmond Hill, Ontario, Canada.

Please send me the following book bargains:

NO. OF COPIES	AMT.	IBM #	TITLE	PRICE
....	....	78619	RUSSIAN HOCKEY SECRETS — Anatoli Tarasov. A famous Russian coach describes the training, tactics and psychology of modern Soviet hockey...	$1.50
....	....	78139	SO YOU WANT TO BE A HOCKEY PLAYER — Brian Conacher. A famous Canadian hockey player tells you what it's really like.	$1.25
....	....	78581	PRO HOCKEY 72/73 — Jim Proudfoot. The latest annual edition of The Hockey Fan's Bible.	$1.95
....	....	78034	HOCKEY IS A BATTLE — Punch Imlach & Scott Young. The career of the coach of the Maple Leafs.	$1.25
....	....	78028	HOCKEY DYNASTY — Jack Batten. How Conn Smythe built a million dollar hockey empire.	$1.25
....	....	75632	I PLAY TO WIN — Stan Mikita. A veteran player tells the story of his hockey battles.	.75

TOTAL
AMOUNT ....

PLUS 25¢ HANDLING CHARGE

TOTAL
ENCLOSED ....PLEASE SEND CHEQUE OR MONEY ORDER. WE ARE NOT RESPONSIBLE FOR ORDERS CONTAINING CASH.

NAME ....

ADDRESS ....

CITY .... PROVINCE ....

THE LOVELIEST AND THE BEST

A love story of brave men and beautiful women.

*   *   *

A love story actually lived by millions of men and women.

*   *   *

THE LOVELIEST AND THE BEST

A story of men who measured their combat lives in minutes . . .
and women who measured their happiness in terms of feverish furloughs
sometimes with their husbands, sometimes with the men they loved.

*   *   *

THE LOVELIEST AND THE BEST

One of the most beautiful, poignant and haunting books to emerge

from World War Two — because this was the way it really happened.

*   *   *

One of a series of original Canadian
POCKET BOOKS

first published by

SIMON & SCHUSTER OF CANADA LIMITED

225 Yonge Street North, Richmond Hill, Ontario.

▼   **AT YOUR BOOKSTORE OR MAIL THE COUPON BELOW**   ▼

RP 33/1